A HISTORY OF HINDI LITERATURE

A HISTORY OF
HINDI
LITERATURE

F. E. KEAY

ISBN : 978-93-5324-559-7 (HB)

First Published, 1920

Published, 2020

Published by

Facsimile Publisher
12 Pragati Market
Ashok Vihar, Ph-2
Delhi-110052
E-mail: books@facsimilepublisher.com

Printed at: G. Print Process, Delhi.

A History of Hindi Literature

Author: F. E. KEAY

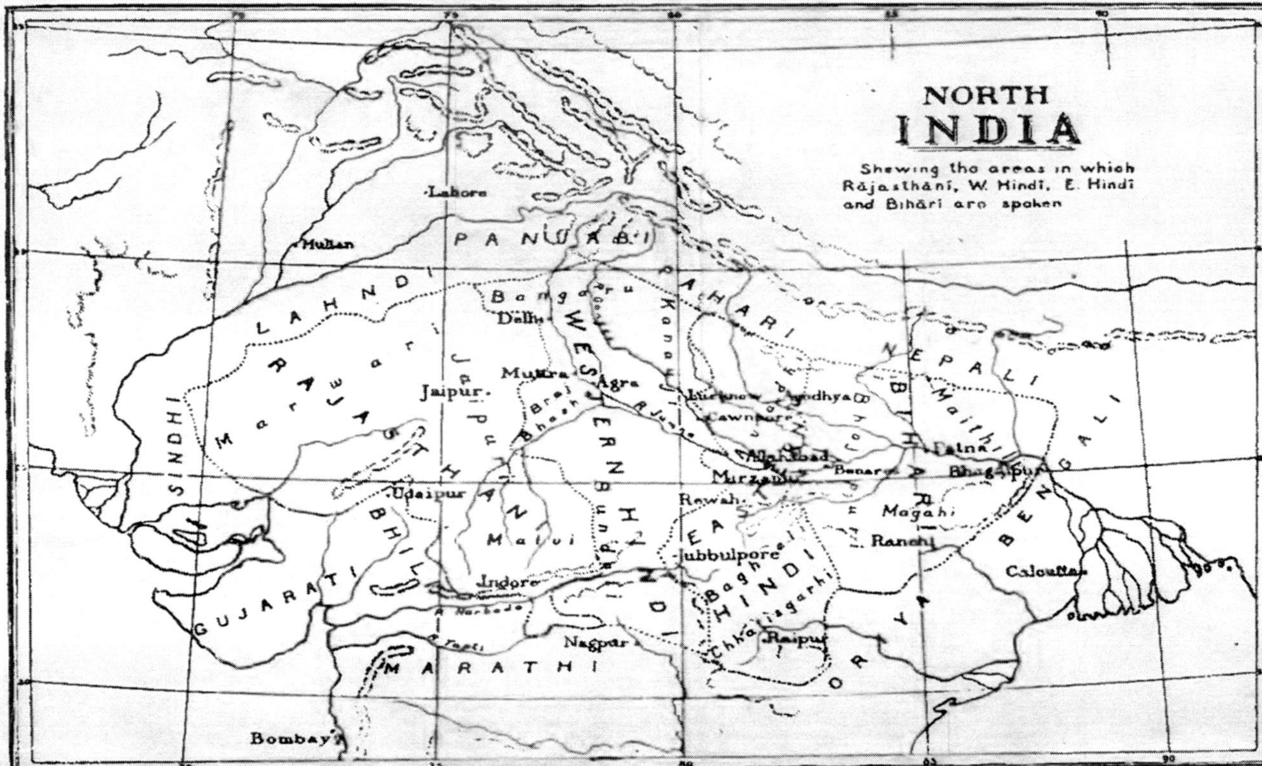
NORTH
INDIA
Shewing the areas in which Rājasthānī, W. Hindī, E. Hindī and Bihārī are spoken
Lahore
Multan
PANJABI
LAHNDI
SINDHI
RAJASTHANI
Marwari
Jaipur
Jaipuri
Malvi
BHIL
GUJARATI
Udaipur
Indore
R. Narbada
R. Tapti
MARATHI
Bombay
Nagpur
Delhi
Bangaru
Mutra
Agra
Braj Bhasha
Kanauji
Bundeli
WESTERN HINDI
PAHARI
NEPALI
Lucknow
Ajodhya
Cawnpore
Allahabad
Mirzapur
Benares
Bhojpuri
Rewah
Jubbulpore
Baghelī
EASTERN HINDI
Chhattisgarhi
Raipur
BIHARI
Maithili
Patna
Bhagalpur
Magahi
Ranchi
BENGALI
Calcutta
ORIYA

CONTENTS

PREFACE

THE purpose of these volumes of The Heritage of India Series on the vernacular literatures is to provide, in each case, a clear and trustworthy outline of the history of the literature. Necessarily, nothing more can be compressed into a hundred pages; and, when one of the greater literatures comes under review, it is impossible, within the limits, to do justice to the whole. In this volume, great care has been taken to sketch the historic movements down to the time of Hariśchandra; but no attempt has been made to give a detailed account of more recent literature.

Amongst the many persons who have supplied information, or given other help, I must especially thank the Editors of this Series; the Rev. G. J. Dann, who kindly read the book in manuscript and offered valuable criticisms; and the Rev. Dr. W. C. Macdougall and Mr. M. T. Kennedy, who have carefully read through the proofs. I am also much indebted to Mr. Kallu Singh and Mr. Sakhawat Masih, masters of my own school, for help in translating some of the extracts.

FRANK E. KEAY.

Jubbulpore: August, 1920.

I.

THE HINDĪ LANGUAGE AND ITS NEIGHBOURS.

The Indo-Aryan Languages.—The Indo-Aryan languages form one branch of the great Indo-European family of languages, which are now spoken over Europe and a large part of Western and Southern Asia. Somewhere near the borderland of Europe and Asia lived the people who spoke the original language from which these various languages have been derived. One great class of this people, called the Aryans, migrated eastwards towards the Oxus, but as they advanced further were split up into two sections, and their language also developed on two different lines. One of these two forms of language became the parent of the Iranian family of languages (Medic, Pahlavi, Persian, etc.). The other branch of the Aryan people pushed on into the valley of the Kaḅul, and thence into the plains of North India. The migration of these peoples was spread over a long period of time. Those who came into India are known as Indo-Aryans. The Indo-Aryan language received a literary culture in quite ancient times and its literary form became known as Sanskrit, that is the "purified" language. This polished literary dialect became fixed, but the ordinary speech of the people, which is called Prākrit, that is "natural," or "unartificial," gradually changed. Diphthongs and harsh combinations were softened, but the language still remained, like Sanskrit, synthetic. The dialects of different areas began to differ more and more from one another. Some of the older forms of the Prākrits meanwhile, like Sanskrit, became fixed and received literary culture, such for instance as Pāli. In the last stage of the Prākrits, before the modern Indo-Aryan languages developed from them, they are known as Apabhraṁśas. These are the direct parents of the modern vernaculars of North India, namely, Hindī, Punjābī, Marāṭhī, etc., which came into existence somewhere about 1000 A.D., though the date differs considerably in the case of different languages. These modern languages are no longer synthetic but analytic.

Hindi.—It is most important to understand clearly what we mean by Hindī, as the word is often used ambiguously. It is often, for instance, applied in a loose sense to the vernacular speech of the whole of North India between the Punjab and Sindh on the West, and Bengal on the East. But the philological researches of scholars, such as Sir George Grierson, have shown that there are really four chief languages in this area, namely, Rājasthānī, Western Hindī, Eastern Hindī, and Bihārī, each having a different parentage. Bihārī really belongs to a group of languages of which Bengalī is another member. Western Hindī is closely connected in origin with Panjābī. The word Hindī is also often used to denote modern literary High Hindī in contradistinction to Urdu; but both High Hindī and Urdu were, as will be shown below, developed from a dialect of Western Hindī. Hindūstāni (or Hindostānī) is also a name used sometimes to denote the vernaculars of all Hindūstān, that is the country between the Punjab and Sindh and Bengal, but is also sometimes used to mean the simpler speech which is the *lingua franca* of modern India, and of which both Urdu and High Hindī are literary developments.

Scope of this Book.—The literature whose history will be described in this book will include Rājasthānī, Western Hindī, Eastern Hindī, and Bihārī literature but not Urdu. It may seem at first sight somewhat arbitrary to group together the literatures of these languages which are believed to have been distinct in development, and when Western Hindī, for instance, is more closely connected in origin with Punjābī, and Bihārī with Bengalī, than with the other languages here grouped with them. Moreover Urdu, whose literature is here excluded, is developed from a dialect of Western Hindī. But the justification for grouping these literatures together lies in this, that whereas Punjābī and Bengalī and Urdu have developed modern literatures which are proceeding each on its own lines, the languages whose literary history is contained in this book have become closely connected in their literary development. In the areas where they are spoken "High Hindī" has come to be accepted as a literary language by almost all those who do not use Urdu, and though the older vernaculars are still used for poetical compositions, not one of them is developing a separate prose literature of its own. Moreover, though considered by scholars as distinct, they are closely related languages which have mutually influenced each other, and the literature of any one of these vernaculars is to a large extent understood by those who speak one of the others. These languages are spoken by over a hundred million people.

As the literature dealt with in the following pages is really connected with distinct though cognate languages it is more accurate to describe it, as Sir George Grierson has done, as the "Modern Vernacular Literature of Hindostān." But for the sake of convenience and to avoid circumlocution it will generally be referred to here as "Hindī Literature." The bulk of it is written in Western Hindī or Eastern Hindī. Bihārī literature is not very extensive and, except for the lyrics of Vidyāpati, not very important. Rājasthānī literature mostly consists of bardic chronicles.

Urdu as a literary language has an important point of difference from Hindī in the metres it employs. These follow Persian models, and the substance of Urdu poetry is largely influenced by Persian themes.

Dialects.—The chief dialects of *Rājasthānī* are Mewātī, Mārwāṛī, Jaipurī, and Mālvī. Of these Mārwāṛī is the chief literary dialect. It is also called

Ḍingal, and in this connection is distinguished from Pingal, the name given in Rājputānā to the Braj Bhāshā dialect of Western Hindī, which was also used in this area as a literary dialect.

Western Hindī has as its principal dialects, Bāngarū, to the west of the Ganges in the highlands of the South-Eastern Panjab; Braj Bhāshā, the language spoken in Muttra and the surrounding district, which is the chief dialect of Western Hindī for poetry; Kanaujī (very similar to Braj Bhāshā), which is spoken in the lower part of the central Doab and the country to the north; Bundelī, in Bundelkhaṇḍ and a good portion of the Narbada valley in the Central Provinces; and another dialect spoken in the neighbourhood of Delhi and Meerut. Delhi being for a long time the headquarters of the Muhammadan conquerors of North India, it was from the dialect of this district that the *lingua franca* of the Mughal camp originated. A great many words of Persian and Arabic origin were introduced into this dialect as well as those of Panjābī and Rājasthāni, and the Persian character was used for writing it. The word "Urdu" literally means "Camp." Urdu was the camp language. Muhammadan influence extended its use far and wide, and it eventually became a literary language. Modern "High Hindī" was developed from Urdu by the exclusion of Persian and Arabic words and the substitution of those of pure Indian origin, Sanskrit or Hindī. The name Khari Boli (*i.e.* "pure speech") is sometimes used by Indian scholars both for the original dialect of Delhi and Meerut, and for the modern High Hindī developed by Lallū Ji Lāl; but they are not identical, as will be shown later in a subsequent chapter when the circumstances of the formation of modern literary Hindī are related.

The dialects of *Eastern Hindī*, from North to South are Avadhī, Baghelī, and Chhattīsgaṛhī. Of these the chief literary dialect is Avadhī, spoken in the country of Ayodhyā (Oudh). Avadhī is also known as Baiswārī.

Bihārī has three principal dialects, namely Maithilī, Bhojpurī, and Magahī. Maithilī is the chief literary dialect, and practically all the works which have come down to us are in this dialect. It is spoken in the region which formed the old kingdom of Mithilā, that is in Bihār north of the Ganges.

The Hindi Alphabet and Written Character.—The alphabet used for Hindī and the other languages included with it in this book is the same as that of Sanskrit, and is arranged in the same way, that is on phonetic principles. One or two of the Sanskrit letters are not used however in Hindī. The written character is generally what is the called the Devanāgarī (or Nāgarī), which is also used for Sanskrit. But other forms are also used. Mahājanī (or Sarrāfī) and Baniauṭī are only used in business. They are both modifications of Kāyathī (or Kaithī). This word is from Kāyath, or Kāyasth, the name of the writer-caste amongst the Hindus. Kāyathī character was originally derived from the Devanāgarī by slight alterations which better adapt it to the purpose of writing quickly. It is used chiefly in the Eastern portion of the area with which we are concerned, but even there is not so common as Devanāgarī.

Vocabulary.—The vast majority of words used in the languages we are considering are those which have come down from the original Indo-Aryan language through the long development of the centuries. But in the language of to-day there are often found words which are direct borrowings from Sanskrit. These are called *Tatsama* words ("the same as that") to distinguish them from *Tadbhava* words ("of the nature of that"), which are those that have undergone change in the long process of development. In many cases *Tatsama* and *Tadbhava* forms of the same word or root co-exist in the language, such as *Yogy* and *Jog* ("fit, worthy"). Words have also been borrowed from Persian. We find these even in the works of the great writers such as Tulsī Dās, and though some modern authors affect to write "pure Hindī," few books can be found which do not contain some words of Persian origin. Some Portuguese, and nowadays many English words, have also found their way into the language.

Hindī Prosody.—There is probably no language in which prosody has been more elaborately developed than in Hindī. Its system is derived ultimately from the principles which govern Sanskrit poetry. It does not, like English, depend on accent, but, like the classic poetry of Greece and Rome, is based on the quantity of the syllables, long or short. But rhyme is also used almost universally, and in Hindī poetry a rhyme means that not only the last syllable of a line, but the last two syllables at least, correspond with those of another line. A good deal of liberty is allowed in respect of orthography and even of grammatical construction, but the rules for the various metres are very complicated. The result however in the hands of a skilful poet is the production of poetry the form and rhythm of which has a wonderful charm probably not surpassed in any language. The number of metres recognized in books of Hindī prosody is very large. A few only of the principal ones can be mentioned here. A *dohā* (or *dohrā*) is a couplet each line of which contains twenty-four *mātras* or instants, divided up again into feet according to a recognized plan. A *Mātra* denotes the length of time occupied in the utterance of a short vowel. Long vowels and diphthongs are regarded as consisting of two *mātras*. The *dohā* is the most popular and frequent of all metres. The *sorathā* is an inverted *dohā*, that is the second half of each line of the *dohā* changes place with the first half. The *chaupāī* ranks with the *dohā* in popularity. It consists of four lines, each of which has sixteen *mātras*. Other much-used metres are the *kuṇḍaliyā*, the *chhappai*, the *kāvya*, the *savaiya* and the *kavitta*. Many metres are specially used in the composition of verses which are intended to be sung. In these the same rhyme is often continued throughout all the lines of the poem.

The Family of Indo-Aryan Languages.

(The languages whose literature is described in this book are printed in thick type).

		(*Apabhraṁśas*)		(*Modern Languages*)
Indo-Aryan Language	Prākrits (Vernacular)	Unknown	..	Kāshmīrī
		Unknown	..	Kohistānī
		Unknown	..	Lahndī (Western Panjābī)
		Vrāchadī	..	Sindhī
		Gaurjarī	..	Gujarātī
		Śauraseni	..	Panjābī
				Western Hindi
		Āvantī	..	*Rājasthānī*
				Pahārī
		Ardhamāgadhī		**Eastern Hindi**
		Māgadhī	..	**Bihari**
				Bengālī
				Oṛiyā
				Assamese
		Mahārāṣṭrī	..	Mārāṭhī
	Sanskrit (Literary)			

II.

A GENERAL SURVEY OF HINDĪ LITERATURE

After the death of King Harsha (646 or 647 A.D.), who had built up a large Empire in North India, there was a long period of confusion and disorder. The unity of Indian History is lost until the Muhammadan conquests again restored a government strong enough to become a paramount power. During this period the Rajput clans came into prominence and various Rajput principalities took shape which were destined to play an important part in subsequent history. These kingdoms were often at war with one another, but the inroads of the Muhammadans from the West frequently united them to meet the common foe. Although Kabul, the Punjab, and Sindh had previously fallen into the hands of the Muhammadan invaders, the real conquest of India did not begin till 1175 A.D. when Muhammad Ghori commenced his attacks. In 1191 the Muhammadan progress induced the Hindu Kings to compose their quarrels and form a great confederacy under Prithīrāj (also called Prithvīrāj or Rai Pithorā), the Chauhān ruler of Ajmer and Delhi. The Hindus were at first victorious in a battle at Tarain, but in the following year were defeated in the same place and Prithvīrāj was captured and killed. Delhi was soon occupied and the Muhammadan advance continued till, under Muhammad-bin-Tughlak in 1340, it attained its maximum extent. But though many Hindu kingdoms fell, and many strongholds in Rajputana were captured, the Rajput clans reasserted themselves and were never completely subdued. Many new Kingdoms were set up, and later Muhammadan sovereigns often found it more profitable to make alliances with the Rajput monarchs than to attack them.

It was during this period that the modern vernaculars of India were taking shape, and the earliest modern vernacular literature of Hindūstān appeared in the form of the bardic chronicles of Rajputana. The stirring times in which they lived produced ample themes for the royal bards, and the liberal patronage of monarchs encouraged their labours. Though full of panegyric and embellished with many legends, and therefore not to be taken as sober history, their poems nevertheless are a stirring record of the desperate struggles between the Hindu kingdoms and their Muhammadan invaders, and of the heroism and chivalry which such a period called forth. The greatest name in the literature of this period is that of Chand Bardāī, the bard of Prithvīrāj. Contemporary with Chand was Jagnāyak, while a famous bard of the middle of the fourteenth century was Śārang Dhar, who sang the prowess of the valorous Hammīr, Prince of Ranthambhor.

The rise of the worship of Rāma, which took place about the beginning of the fifteenth century, gave another great impetus to vernacular literature. One branch of Vaishṇavas worshipped Vishṇu under the form of Kṛishṇa and this form of worship had long been popular. Now, largely owing to the great influence of Rāmānanda, others made Rāma their principal object of worship. A later development, due in some measure to Muhammadan influence, and in which Kabīr was the first great teacher, was in the direction of a non-idolatrous theism. All these various movements were part of a great religious revival which was widespread amongst the people, and all began to use the vernacular for their literature. From this time on the vernacular literature was mostly dominated by religious ideals and almost entirely on the lines which had been laid down by the Vaishṇava reformers. This period begins about 1400 and includes such poets as Nāmdev, Kabīr, Vidyāpati, Mīrā Bāī and Malik Muhammad. The earlier bards of Rajputana wrote in a time of transition, using a language which was still full of Prākrit forms, and this was the period of the infancy of Hindī Literature. But when the poets of this next period composed their works, the language spoken was practically the same as the vernacular speech of to-day; and, as the earliest authors in this language, they had to feel their way, for in using the vernacular for their poems they were making a great venture. This was the period of the youth of Hindī Literature.

The golden age of the vernacular literature of Hindūstān begins about 1550. The Mughal sovereigns not only established a strong rule, but were liberal patrons of literature and art. Under Akbar (1556-1605), Jahāngīr (1605-1627) and Shāh Jahān (1627-1658) the Muhammadan rule in India reached its highest point of outward magnificence and this was also the period of the greatest glory in Hindī literature. It has often been pointed out how it synchronizes with the Elizabethan age of English literature, and that at this very time England and India first came into real contact with each other. This period was marked by the introduction of an artistic influence into the literature, leading to a greater polish in versification and form, and the first attempts to systematize the art of poetry by such writers as Keśāv Dās and others. This was the age of the greatest stars of Hindī literature—Tulsī Dās, Sūr Dās and Bihārī Lāl, as well as of other great writers like the Tripāṭhī brothers, Dev Kavi and Senāpati. It was the period when the Sikh *Granth* was compiled and when many new sects were formed, like the Dādūpanthīs, which produced a great deal of religious verse of a high order. The end of the period however, during the eighteenth century, coinciding with the time of the decay of the Mughal Empire, was a time of decline in the high quality of Hindī literature, and does not contain many writers of first-rate excellence.

At the beginning of the nineteenth century a new influence came into Hindī literature through contact with the culture of Europe. In the eighteenth century the English had been struggling in India with the French for mastery, but now that conflict had been decided and the English supremacy was further established by the break up of the old Mughal Empire and the weakening of the Marāṭhā power. English influence now began to make itself more and more felt in Indian affairs, and amongst other things the contact of India with the culture of the West had the effect of stimulating many new ideas, while the sense of security which freedom from internal disorder gave, encouraged the native genius of India to reassert itself. Hence there began about this time a mighty literary renascence in India which is still in progress. At the beginning of this period Lallū Jī Lāl laid the foundation of modern Hindī prose and also created the literary dialect which was to be its principal medium. The printing-press now began to spread literature far and wide. The revival of Hindī poetry was led by Hariśchandra, and this period saw also the rise of the Hindī drama.

The principle adopted in this book in dividing up the literature into periods is as follows. First of all the infancy of Hindī literature, connected with the bardic chronicles, is described; and after that a new period is dated from each point where an important new influence begins to modify the literature. These periods begin (1) about 1400, when the religious influence of the Vaishṇava movements began to affect Hindī literature; (2) about 1550, when a new artistic influence makes itself felt; and (3) about 1800, when the literature began to be affected by the modern influence which came from contact with the West. In each period the literature that shows the new spirit in its fulness will first of all be described and then the other forms in turn, and something will be said as to how far each group or each writer is influenced by the new ideas.

III.

EARLY BARDIC CHRONICLES (1150-1400)

The Earliest Poets.—During the time when the Rajput clans were establishing their power, and while they were struggling with the Muhammadan invaders, every court had its bards who celebrated in song the valour and heroism of their patrons and their race. These bards belonged to guilds, which were also castes, and there are said to have been Chāraṇas, Bhāṭas, Sevagas and Pancholis. The Chāraṇas and Bhāṭas both claimed Brahmanic descent. The language used at first by these bards must have been the local Prākrit, but gradually the Prākrit developed into the modern vernacular. A number of bards are mentioned by tradition as having composed poems between 700 and 1150 A.D. The chief of these are *Pushya* (or *Puṇḍa*), *Kedar*, *Ananya Dās*, *Masaud*, *Qutub Ali* and *Akaram Faiz*. Their work, however, has not survived and it is therefore impossible to say whether the language they used is to be reckoned as Prākrit or as the modern vernacular. A poetic chronicle of the ruling family of Mewār, called the *Khumān Rāsā*, which dates from the sixteenth century, is said to have been founded on a work written in the ninth century, but no fragment of the original has survived. In 1143 a certain Kumār Pāl became king of Gujarāt, his capital being at Anhilwār. In 1159, under the influence of the Jain scholar Hemachandra he became a Jain, and at a rather late date Hemachandra wrote a romantic poem in Prākrit entitled *Kumāra Pāla Charitra*. An anonymous bardic chronicle, called by the same name, in the early speech of the modern vernacular is said to date from the middle of the thirteenth century, and is probably a free adaptation of the Prākrit poem. Vīsala Deva (Bīsal Dev) was the king of Ajmer in 1001 A.D. when Mahmūd of Ghaznī made one of his raids into India. He is celebrated in a short poem called *Bīsal Dev Rāso*, the date of which is unknown, but which has been considered by some to belong to the thirteenth century. Till these poems are dated and their language thoroughly examined by scholars, it is not possible to say what evidence they give as to the date when the modern vernacular became clearly distinguished from the earlier Prākrit, and as even the *Prithī Rāj Rāso*, which is dated in 1191, is said by such an eminent authority as Sir George Grierson to be "abounding in pure Apabhraṁśa Śauraśenī Prākrit forms," it would be rash in the absence of further evidence to place the date of the emergence of the modern vernaculars of Hindūstān much earlier than the beginning of the twelfth century.

Chand Bardai.—Prithī Rāj (also called Prithvī Rāj or Rai Pithorā), who was born 1159 and killed in 1192, was the Chauhān ruler of Ajmer and Delhi at the time of the battles of Tarain, in the second of which he was captured and afterwards slain. He was a great patron of literature, and besides Ananya Dās, mentioned above, his court was also attended by the famous bard *Chand Bardāī*. Chand Bardāī belonged to an old family of bards, and the famous poet Sūr Dās is said by some to have been one of his descendants. He came to the court of Prithī Rāj and was appointed as his minister and poet-laureate. His poetical works were collected by Amar Singh of Mewār in the seventeenth century, and it is probable that they were then recast and partially modernized though still full of archaic language. Chand's chief work is the *Prithī Rāj Rāso*. In this famous poem of sixty-nine books and 100,000 stanzas he gives the life of his patron and the history of the time in which he wrote. Chand Bardāī and his patron were both killed after the battle of Tarain in 1192. Legend and fiction are mixed up with history in the *Prithī Rāj Rāso.* The repeated conflicts related to have taken place between Prithī Rāj and Sultān Shihabuddīn seem to be quite unhistorical, and the Mughals are brought on the stage thirty years before they really appeared in Indian History. It is therefore doubtful whether the document in its entirety is a contemporary poem, but the language used, which is transitional in character and abounds in strange forms which have long since ceased to be used, makes it seem likely that the original core of the poem is certainly the work of Chand Bardāī, and that it is one of the earliest poems in Hindī which have survived. Owing to the difficulty of the language it is a poem not easy to read even for scholars, but those who have studied it have a high opinion of its literary merits. It is of immense value from the point of view of linguistic study.

The following lines are taken from the twentieth book of Chand's epic. The fair Padmāvatī, daughter of Padam Sen, an opponent of Prithī Rāj, had heard of the nobility of Prithīrāj, as he had of her beauty, and when her marriage was arranged with another, she sent a message by a parrot to Prithīrāj to come and rescue her. Prithīrāj came with an army to seize her as his bride :—

" Watching the road in the direction of Delhi,
Happy was she when the parrot returned,
Hearing the news, glad were her eyes ;
The maiden was elated with the tokens of love,
She tore off the dirty clothes from her body,
Purified, and anointed, and adorned herself with robes,
Called for priceless jewels (for her person) from head to foot,
Arrayed with the tokens of the king of love.
Filling a golden tray with pearls,
Lighting a lamp she waved it round,
Taking her confidante with her, boldly the maiden
Goes as Rukmini went to meet Murāri ;
Worshipping Gaurī, revering Śankar ;
Circumambulating and touching their feet.
Then on seeing King Prithīrāj,
She smiled bashfully, hiding her face through shame.
Seizing her hand, putting her on horseback,

The King, the Lord of Delhi, took her away.
The rumour spıead that, outside the city,
They are carrying off Padmāvatī by force.
Drums are beat, there is saddling of horse and elephant,
They ran, armed, in all directions.
'Seize! Seize!' shouted each warrior.
Rage possessed the heroes and their king.
When King Prithīrāj was going in front
With all his army behind him,
There the horsemen advancing arrived;
King meeting King, the warriors joined in battle,
When Prithīrāj the King turns rein,
The heavens stand still, the world-serpent shakes.
The chiefs and heroes all look (awful) as death,
Eager for blood on rushes the King,
The bows let fly countless arrows,
The deadly blades draw blood.
From the sweat of the wounds of the heroes on the field,
A thick stream flows, and dyes the sand,
As warriors of the *barāt* smote,
On the field fell heads and headless trunks of the foe.
The foe fell on the field of battle;
Turning his face towards Delhi,
Having won the battle, went Prithīrāj,
All the chiefs were glad.
He took Padmāvatī with him
Rejoicing, King Prithīrāj."[1]

Chand Bardāī's son *Jalhan* is also said to have been a poet and possibly some parts of the *Rāso* were composed by him.

Jagnayak.—*Jagnāyak* (or *Jagnik*) was a contemporary of Chand Bardāī and attended the court of Paramardī (Parmāl) of Mahobā in Bundelkhaṇḍ, who was a rival of Prithīrāj. His works have not survived, unless we have in the *Mahobā Khaṇḍ* (or *Ālhā Khaṇḍ*), which has been described as a spurious canto of Chand's epic, a poem which was written by Jagnāyak. This poem has been handed down by oral tradition and exists in many recensions which differ from one another both in language and subject matter. It is still sung by professional singers in India and the language is always modernized to suit the dialect of the reciter.

[1] Translation by Mr. John Beames, in Vol. 38 of the Journal of the Asiatic Society of Bengal (1869), pp. 152, 153.

The heroes of this poem are Ālhā and Ūdal (or Ūdan). Portions of one recension have been translated into English ballad metre by Mr. Waterfield, under the title of "The Nine-Lakh Chain or the Maro Feud." A few stanzas will give some idea of this poem. It relates Ālhā's victory over King Jambay :—

The warriors staggered, they scattered and broke,
In hope their lives to save;
When Jambay saw they fled, he spoke,
And his elephant onward drave.

"Mahobā's champion, Devi's son,
Now settle thy cause with me;
Alive from the field shall go but one,
So turn by turn strike we."

"I may not strike, by the Chandel law;
Do thou strike first, O King";
Then a good red bow did Jambay draw,
And fitted the notch to string.

The aim was good, the string did twang,
Fast did the arrow fly;
Across the howda Ālhā sprang,
And the shaft went whizzing by.

Then his javelin flew as near they drew,
Now how may Ālhā bide?
Queen Sārada's care at his right hand there
She turned the spear aside.

"Now hear, Banāphar," Jambay spake,
"Twice hast thou foiled my blow;
In peace thy way to Mahobā take,
For thrice thou 'scap'st not so."

But Ālhā there his breast made bare,
And did to the Rājā cry;
"No part of a Kshatrī's trade it were,
From the battle trench to fly."

"There are homes in heaven stand ready for all,
To-morrow if not to-day;
And if in Māro this tide shall fall,
My name shall live for aye."

"One chance is left thee, King, to save,
And see thou miss no more":
Then drew the King his shining glaive,
And thrice he smote full sore.

No hurt on Ālhā's body happ'd,
His shield was lifted high;
At length the sword of Jambay snapp'd,
Then wist he death was nigh.

'I have hewn down elephants with this blade,
And lopped their limbs away;
Its master's need has it now betrayed,
My life is lost to-day!"

"Now, Rājā, now my stroke take thou,"
And his elephant on he drove;
Howda to howda, tusk to tusk,
Close met the champions strove.

Then Ālhā forward dash'd his shield,
With the boss he dealt a blow;
The elephant's driver was hurl'd to the field,
And he waver'd to and fro.

Then Jambay drew his dagger keen,
Long time their steel they plied;
On Ālhā's body no hurt was seen,
"Now bind the foe," he cried.

Pachsawad whirl'd his iron chain,
Dashed the howda to the ground;
Soon Ālhā lighted on the plain,
And fast his arms he bound.[1]

Sarang Dhar.—*Śārang Dhar*, a bard who flourished in the middle of the fourteenth century, is said to have been a descendant of Chand Bardāi. He is the reputed author of two poems known as the *Hammīr Rāsā* and the *Hammīr Kāvya*, which are chronicles of the royal house of Ranthambhor. The valour of Hammīr in his struggle against the emperor Alā-ud-dīn, at whose hands he received his death, is very famous. Śārang Dhar is also the author of an anthology of Sanskrit lyric stanzas called the *Śārngadhara Paddhati*, which was published in 1363.

These early bards had a long line of successors, some of whom will be mentioned later on. Their chronicles are valuable not only as literature, but as a record of the times in which they lived. Like the old

[1] Calcutta Review, Vol. 63 (1876), pp. 414 ff.

chronicles of other lands they contain much that is legendary and unreliable as history, but the light which they throw on the period in which they were written is nevertheless of very great value.

Other Poets of this Period.—One or two other writers who are considered to belong to this period may also be mentioned. These are *Bhūpati*, who wrote at the end of the thirteenth century, and *Nalla Singh*, *Mullā Dāūd*, and *Amīr Khusro*, who flourished about the fourteenth century. The latter was a Persian poet to whom Hindī verses are also ascribed. There is also a certain Gorakhnāth who is regarded as the founder of an order of Yogīs, and as the author of both Sanskrit and Hindī works. Some doubt has been expressed as to his being a historical person at all, but it seems likely that he was, and that he lived about 1200 A.D. The Hindī works, which include one in prose, are almost certainly not written by him. They are probably the works of his followers. They have been placed by some as early as the middle of the fourteenth century, but their date at present must be regarded as very uncertain.

IV.

EARLY BHAKTI POETS (1400-1550)

The Vaishnava Revival.—A new development in Hindī literature was caused by the growth of the Vaishṇava movement in North India. The Muhammadan conquest had been a time of great difficulty for the Hindu religion. Scholars had been dispersed, idols broken, and temples cast down. But though Hinduism suffered severely it was not destroyed, and a great impetus was to be given to the Vaishṇava form of the Hindu faith. The Vaishṇava religious movements of North India at this time fall into three groups, Rāmaite, Kṛishṇaite, and deistic. But all the various sects have many points in common. A personal God, who is full of love and pity for his devotees, is the object of worship, and towards him devotion *(bhakti)* is demanded as the most important requirement from those who would obtain release. The movement as a whole was a revolt against the cold intellectualism of Brahmanic philosophy and the lifeless formalism of mere ceremonial. It was essentially a popular religious movement, and this is emphasised by its use of the vernacular, rather than Sanskrit, in the vast amount of literature it produced. This constitutes the importance of the movement from the point of view of Hindī literature.

Ramananda's Predecessors.—It is generally agreed that it was Rāmānanda who gave the greatest impulse to the religious revival in North India about this time, but there were others who were his predecessors and the harbingers of the movement. The *Ādi Granth* of the Sikhs, compiled by Guru Arjun in 1604, has preserved some of the earliest specimens we possess of Hindī poetry of the *bhakti* movement. Among those devotees (*bhagats*) of whose compositions fragments have been preserved in the *Granth*, and who are earlier than Rāmānanda, are Sadnā and Nāmdev. The *Granth* contains also a fragment of a certain *Jaidev* who has sometimes been identified with Jayadeva, the author of the Sanskrit *Gītā Govinda*, who lived towards the end of the twelfth century. But the identification is more than doubtful and the date and the circumstances of this Jaidev are unknown.

Sadnā, who probably flourished about the beginning of the fifteenth century, is said to have been born in Sindh and to have been a butcher (*kasāī*). He gave up his trade and became a devotee. Only a couple of his hymns are preserved in the *Granth.*

Nāmdev belonged to the Marāṭhā country and was a devotee of Viṭhobā at Paṇḍharpūr. He probably flourished between about 1400 and 1430. By caste he was a tailor, and according to the legends preserved about him he showed great devotion in his boyhood, but afterwards for a time lived an evil life in company with a band of dacoits. He repented, however, and became a great devotee. He is the author of a considerable number of Marāṭhī hymns, but he was a noteworthy religious leader in the north of India also, and wrote many verses in Hindī. A considerable number of hymns composed by him are in the *Granth.* Nāmdev is a most interesting figure and probably one of the first leaders of the new religious revival which began about this time in North India.

Ramananda, who lived probably from about 1400 to 1470, was an ascetic who somewhere about the year 1430 began to preach that the eternal God should be worshipped under the name of Rāma, that Rāma alone was the source of release from the evils of transmigration, and that this should be sought by fervent devotion (*bhakti*) towards him. The way had already been prepared by the preaching of others on similar lines, and Rāmānanda evidently met with such success that he took up his residence in Benares and made that the headquarters of the new movement. He was undoubtedly one of the most important Hindu religious leaders in North India, for not only is the sect of Rāmānandīs, which acknowledges him as its direct founder, still very large, but a great many other sects owe their first impulse to the movement he initiated, or else were founded by those who were originally his disciples or members of his sect. As a writer, however, Rāmānanda does not hold an important place. Hymns in Hindī purporting to have been written by him are still preserved, one of them in the *Ādi Granth.* In this hymn he seems to be declining an invitation to go and worship Vishṇu in a temple, on the ground that God is all-pervading and that he has found God in his heart. It must not be inferred from this, however, that Rāmānanda forbade idolatry though he may have criticised it. He preached a vivid faith in the reality of the one personal God, spiritual and invisible, whom he called Rāma, but no break was made with idolatry, the Hindu pantheon, or the old mythology. Nor did Rāmānanda throw over the system of caste. It is true that like other *bhakti* teachers before his day he was willing to acknowledge that even outcastes, by means of *bhakti*, could obtain release, and that amongst his personal disciples there are said to have been not a only a Śūdra, a Jāt, and an outcaste, but even a Muhammadan weaver and a woman. But there is no evidence that he modified the social rules of caste in the slightest. From the point of view of Hindī literature the significance of the movement initiated by Rāmānanda was in depending for its literature almost entirely on the vernacular. The followers and successors of Rāmānanda practically gave up the use of Sanskrit, and this of course gave a great impetus to the development of Hindī literature.

Ramananda's Disciples.—The immediate personal disciples of Rāmānanda were, according to tradition, twelve in number, and Hindī compositions of some of these have been preserved. *Pīpā* was the Rājā of Gagaraungaṛh and is said to have been born in the year 1425. On becoming a disciple of Rāmānanda he abdicated his sovereignty and became a mendicant. *Dhanā*, the Jāt, is said to have been born in 1415. *Sen* was a barber at the court of the Rājā of Rewah. Of these three disciples of Rāmānanda only a few hymns have been preserved in the *Ādi Granth*. *Bhawānand*, another disciple, is the reputed author of an explanation in Hindī of the Vedānta system of philosophy in fourteen chapters called the *Amrit Dhār*. *Rai Dās* was the *chamār* disciple of Rāmānanda, and attained great celebrity as a devotee. More than thirty of his hymns have been preserved in the *Ādi Granth*. The following, in which he describes his relation to God, is a specimen:—

"If Thou art a hill, then I am Thy peacock;
If Thou art the moon, then I am Thy *chakor;*
O God, if Thou break not with me, I will not break with
Thee;
If I break with Thee, whom shall I join?
If Thou art a lamp, then I am Thy wick;
If Thou art a place of pilgrimage, then I am Thy pilgrim.
I have joined true love with Thee;
Joining Thee I have broken with all others.
Wherever I go there is Thy service;
There is no other Lord like Thee, O God.
By worshipping Thee Death's noose is cut away.
Rav Dās singeth to obtain Thy service."[1]

Kabir.—The greatest of the disciples of Rāmānanda, whether as a poet or a religious leader, was the Muhammadan weaver Kabīr (1440-1518). According to legend he was really the son of a Brahman widow, who, in order to conceal her shame, exposed the infant in the Lahar Tank near Benares, where it was discovered by Nīrū, the Muhammadan weaver, and his wife Nīmā, and brought up by them as their own child. Another version gives an entirely miraculous account of his birth. Even as a boy he is said to have given offence both to Hindus and Muhammadans. The former he angered by putting on a sacred cord though of low caste, and the latter by using Hindu names for God

[1] Macauliffe, "The Sikh Religion," Vol. VI. p. 331.

though he was a Muhammadan. He was taunted also with being a *nigura*, that is one without a *guru*. Desiring to remove this reproach he wished to become a disciple of Rāmānanda, but feared that he might not be accepted. He therefore had recourse to a stratagem. Lying down upon the steps of the *ghāṭ* which he knew Rāmānanda visited, he hoped that in the dark the *guru* might stumble over him, and that probably then no words would rise so readily to his lips as the *mantra* of his order. This hope was realised and Rāmānanda uttered the words "Rām, Rām." Kabīr claimed that he had been initiated and Rāmānanda admitted the claim. After this initiation Kabīr is said to have visited his *guru* regularly, but though a disciple of Rāmānanda he went far beyond his master in his teaching. Whether he was originally a Muhammadan or not, there is no doubt that Muhammadan influence can be traced in his ideas. He was the founder of the deistic movement in India. He uses the name Rāma for God (as well as other names such as Hari, Govind, Allāh, etc.) and has Vedāntic ideas, but he rejected entirely the doctrine of incarnations, and with no unsparing voice condemned idolatry and most of the Hindu ceremonies and rites. The influence of Kabīr, both direct and indirect, has been enormous. Not only is the sect of Kabīrpanthīs, which claims him as its founder, still very numerous, but many other sects owe to him the leading ideas of their theology. Many of these sects will be mentioned later on in connection with the literature which their leaders produced. There are many legends but not very much reliable information about the life of Kabīr. His interest in religious questions to the neglect of his weaving seems to have brought him sometimes into conflict with his family, but even more trouble came to him from the opposition of both Hindus and Muhammadans, who were offended in turn at his denunciation of many of their practices. He seems to have been persecuted by the Emperor Sikandar Lodī, after being denounced by both Hindus and Muhammadans as a troublesome person, and finally was exiled from Benares by the Emperor's orders. He went to live at Maghar in the Gorakhpur district, where he ended his days.

The poems composed by Kabīr are very numerous. It is probable that he himself did not commit them to writing, but that they were remembered and treasured up by his disciples. Various collections of poems ascribed to Kabīr have come down to us, but there is a strong probability that there is much in these collections that is not his genuine work. One collection is to be found in the *Ādi Granth* of the Sikhs, which was compiled in 1604. Another collection is contained in the *Bījak* (literally "invoice," or "account-book," or perhaps "a document by which a hidden treasure can be located"). This work was produced in connection with the Kabīr Panth after the death of Kabīr probably as a book of instruction. It is often said to have been compiled by Bhago Dās, one of Kabīr's immediate disciples, about the year 1570. The *Bījak* is a collection of verses in various metres. The *Ramaiṇīs* are short doctrinal poems. The *Śabdas* are similar but in a different metre. The *Chauntīsā* is an exposition of the religious signification of the consonants of the Nāgarī alphabet. In the thirty verses of the *Vipramatīsī* an attack is made on the orthodox system of the Brahmans. The *Kaharās*, *Vasantas*, *Belīs*, *Chāncharīs*, *Birhūlīs* and *Hiṇḍolās* are religious verses in the metres so named. The collection ends with over four hundred Sākhīs, or short apophthegms, each consisting of a single *dohā*, and the *Sāyar Bījak Ko Pad*, which sums up the whole matter. Neither the verses contained in the *Ādi Granth* nor those in the *Bījak* can be regarded in their entirety as the work of Kabīr. Besides these there are a very large number of Sākhīs (of which over five thousand have been collected) and other verses ascribed to Kabīr which are still current in India. At the Kabīr Chaurā, which is the headquarters of the Kabīr Panth at Benares, there is said to be a collection of the works of Kabīr, called the *Khās Granth*, which includes about twenty different books.

Many of these are evidently the works of disciples or successors, though few of them have been published. The dialect used in the compositions contained in the Bījak is the old Avadhī dialect of Hindī. The poetry of Kabīr is rough and unpolished, and the style and language make it not always easy to understand. Words are often loosely strung together with very little regard to grammatical accuracy, and the sentences are often elliptical and full of colloquialisms. The frequent play on words and the obscurity of many of the similes used increase the difficulty. But in spite of all this Kabīr must be given a very high place in Hindī literature. The amazing boldness with which he attacked the religious practices of his day, tolerating no shams and demanding reality in all those who were seeking after God, and the moral earnestness of his appeal to men to put the things of God first, would in itself give his work an outstanding importance. But besides this the stinging satire which he has at his command, and his ability to produce striking epigrams, and the fascinating rhythm of his verse, all combine to give a wonderful power to his poetry. He has been called the pioneer of Hindī literature and the father of all Hindī hymns; but though, in view of the predecessors we have already mentioned, such a claim can hardly be allowed, it is certainly true to say that it was he more than any others before him who popularized Hindī religious literature and vastly extended its influence, and Hindī literature of the same type subsequent to Kabīr owes to him a great debt.

Translations of his poems give very little idea of the charm and force of his style, but a few extracts may help to give some idea of the kind of literature he produced. Here are one or two of the *Sākhīs* ascribed to him:—

> " Everything is from God and nothing from His servant;
> He can change a mustard-seed into a mountain and a mountain into a mustard-seed."

> " The house of God is distant, as is a tall palm;
> He who climbs to the top, tastes of heaven; he who falls is ground in pieces."

"Consider the parable of the sieve; it suffers the flour to pass, but retains the husk;
So men let pass what is good and swallow what is useless."[1]

The lines below illustrate Kabīr's theological standpoint:—

If God be within the mosque, then to whom does this world belong?
If Rām be within the image which you find upon your pilgrimage, then who is there to know what happens without?
Hari is in the East; Allāh is in the West. Look within your heart, for there you will find both Karīm and Rām;
All the men and women of the world are His living forms.
Kabīr is the child of Allāh and of Rām: He is my guru, He is my Pir."[2]

One more extract will illustrate the poetical merit of Kabīr's verse:—

No one knew the mystery of that weaver: who came into the world and spread the warp.
The earth and sky are the two beams: the sun and moon are two filled shuttles.
Taking a thousand threads he spreads them lengthways: to-day he weaveth still, but hard to reach is the far-off end.
Says Kabir, Joining Karma with Karma, woven with unwoven threads, splendidly the weaver weaves.[3]

The son of Kabīr, named *Kamāl*, is also said to have been a poet, and his couplets to have been made in refutation of the sayings of his father whom he seems to have opposed. Hence arose the proverb, "An unlucky family was Kabīr's, in which the son Kamāl was born."

Nanak.—Of the many movements which owe their inspiration to the teaching of Kabīr none is more important than the religion of the Sikhs, which was founded in the Punjab by Nānak (1469-1538). It is said that Nānak, when twenty-seven years of age, met Kabīr, and the influence of the latter is seen not only in the large number of Kabīr's compositions afterwards included in the Sikh *Granth*, but in the doctrines of Nānak, which are very similar to those of Kabīr, and

[1] Translations from Westcott's "Kabīr and the Kabīr Panth," pp. 95, 86, 93.

[2] Translation by Sir Rabindranath Tagore, "Kabir's Poems," 69.

[3] *Bījak*. Ramaiṇī 28. (Rev. Ahmad Shāh's translation.)

undoubtedly owe a great deal to him, though Nānak stands nearer to Hinduism than Kabīr. Nānak made journeys in several directions accompanied by his disciple Mardana, who played the rebeck while Nānak sang. His hymns and other poetical utterances were in a mixture of Punjābi and Hindī. Although he is not equal to Kabīr as a poet, yet his verse is clear and pithy, and not lacking in poetical excellence. Nānak soon gathered a number of followers and one of his most famous compositions is the *Japjī*, a collection of verses which he arranged for their daily use in praise and prayer. Besides this he composed a very large number of other verses which are included in the Sikh *Granth*. The following is one verse from the *Japjī*:—

> "There is no limit to God's praises; to those who repeat them there is no limit.
> There is no limit to His mercy, and to His gifts there is no limit.
> There is no limit to what God seeth, no limit to what He heareth.
> The limit of the secret of His heart cannot be known.
> The limit of His creation cannot be known; neither His near nor His far side can be discovered.
> To know His limits how many vex their hearts.
> His limits cannot be ascertained;
> Nobody knoweth His limits.
> The more we say, the more there remains to be said.
> Great is the Lord, and exalted is His seat.
> His exalted name is higher than the most exalted.
> Were any one else ever so exalted,
> Then He would know that exalted Being:
> How great He is He knoweth Himself.
> Nānak, God bestoweth gifts on whom He looketh with favour and mercy."[1]

The Krishna Cult.—The followers of Rāmānanda, as well as those of Kabīr and Nānak, generally gave the name of Rāma to the Supreme God, though other names were sometimes used. The followers of Rāmānanda accepted Rāma as an incarnation, and permitted idolatry, but the doctrine of incarnation and the use of images were both rejected by Kabīr and Nānak. It was indeed still *bhakti* to Rāma which they

[1] *Japji*, XXIV; Translation by Macauliffe, "The Sikh Religion," Vol. I. 208.

preached, but to Rāma as the invisible God, not as an incarnation. There was however another group of Vaishṇavas who worshipped God under the form of another incarnation, namely Kṛishṇa. Like the Rāmaite cult the worship of Kṛishṇa also had its beginnings in the centuries before this period, but about this time received a new impetus, which was marked, as well as furthered, by the use of the vernacular for its religious literature. Sometimes it was the child Kṛishṇa who was especially thought of as an object of worship, but more often it was that aspect of Kṛishṇa's life which was concerned with his relation to Rādhā and the other Gopīs that received most attention.

Rādhā-Kṛishṇaite verse goes back to the Sanskrit *Gītā Govinda* of Jayadeva in the twelfth century, and as early as the fourteenth century Kṛishṇa hymns appeared in Bengālī. Between 1450 and 1480 there flourished a Gujarātī poet named *Narsingh Mehtā* who wrote Rādhā-Kṛishṇa lyrics in that language. He is also credited with having composed similar verses in Hindī.

Vidyāpati Ṭhākur, who lived at Bisapī in the Darbhangā district of Bihār in the middle of the fifteenth century, is one of the most famous Vaishṇava poets of Eastern India. He was the founder of a school of master-singers which afterwards spread all over Bengal. Little is known of his life, but he was the author of several Sanskrit works. His chief fame however rests on his sonnets in the Maithilī dialect of Bihārī. In these he uses the story of the love which Rādhā bore to Kṛishṇa as an allegory to describe the relation of the soul to God. Many of these were afterwards adapted to Bengālī and made popular by Chaitanya, and Vidyāpati has had many imitators. His poems possess great literary merit and he has had a great influence on the literature of the Eastern part of India.

Umāpati was probably a contemporary of Vidyāpati, and also wrote Kṛishṇaite songs both in in Maithilī and in Bengālī.

Mira Bai.—About the same time as Vidyāpati, or perhaps a little later, there flourished in the west of Hiṇdūstān a writer whose poems helped to popularize the Kṛishṇa cult in that region. This was *Mīrā Bāī* (fl. 1470) the most famous of Hindī poetesses. There has been a great deal of confusion as to her date and the details of her life. But it seems that she was a princess of Rajputana who was married to Bhojrāj, the heir-apparent of Kumbha, Mahārāṇā of Mewār. Her husband died before he came to the throne, and Kumbha was put to death by another son Ūdekaran (or Ūda), who seized the throne in 1469. Mīrā Bāī, who was a devotee of Kṛishṇa even from her childhood, seems already to have given offence to the family of her husband by her refusal to conform to their particular form of Hindu worship, and her frequent lavish expenditure in the entertainment of *sādhūs*, and when her brother-in-law Ūdekaran had gained the throne, he persecuted her so much that she fled from Chitor and became a disciple of Rai Dās, the *chamār* disciple of Rāmānanda. This must have been about the year 1470. She is said to have been especially devoted to that form of Kṛishṇa known as Ranchhor, and a legend says that one day while worshipping with great devotion she was taken up into the image and disappeared. Rai Dās, as a follower of Rāmānanda, was a worshipper of Rāma, and it is not clear why Mīrā Bāī chose him as her *guru*, or whether Rai Dās in any way modified her views, but he is mentioned two or three times in the poems ascribed to her. The lyrics of Mīrā Bāī are occupied with intense devotion to Kṛishṇa, though in some of them she uses the name of Rāma also for God. They are written in the Braj Bhāshā dialect and are graceful and melodious verses. There are many similar lyrics in Gujarātī which are also ascribed to Mīrā Bāī. The following is the translation of one of her lyrics :—

> "God (*i.e.* Kṛishṇa) hath entwined my soul, O Mother,
> With His attributes, and I have sung of them.

The sharp arrow of His love hath pierced my body through and through, O Mother.
When it struck me I knew it not; now it cannot be endured, O Mother.
Though I use charms, incantations, and drugs, the pain will not depart.
Is there any one who will treat me? Intense is the agony, O Mother.
Thou, O God, art near; Thou art not distant; come quickly to meet me.
Saith Mīrā, the Lord, the mountain-wielder, who is compassionate, hath quenched the fire of my body, O Mother.
The Lotus-eyed hath entwined my soul with the twine of His attributes."[1]

Vallabhacharya.—The spread of the worship of Kṛishṇa, however, owed most to Vallabhāchārya. He was the son of a Brahman from South India and was born at Benares in 1479. He established an image of Kṛishṇa at Gobardhan in the Braj country, and from this as his headquarters spread the doctrine of his sect in many parts of India. He wrote many works in Sanskrit, but nothing in Hindī, though the movement he initiated has produced many Hindī writers. He died in 1531 and was succeeded as leader of the sect by his son Viṭṭhalnāth.

Viṭṭhalnāth, who lived from about 1515 to 1585, not only became the leader of the sect which his father had founded but is also credited with having been a Hindī writer. Besides Hindī verses the genuineness of which is doubtful, he is also said to have been the author of a short prose work called *Maṇḍan* dealing with the story of Rādhā and Kṛishṇa, which must be one of the earliest extant prose writings in Hindī. It is written in Braj Bhāshā. Four of the disciples of his father Vallabhāchārya, together with four of his own disciples became the celebrated *Ashṭa Chhāp*, who are mentioned in a later chapter.

Divisions of the Bhakti Movement.—During this period (1400-1550) the various *bhakti* movements of Hinduism fall into three groups, namely (1) those who

[1] Translation by Macauliffe, "The Religion of the Sikhs," Vol. VI. 356.

worshipped Rāma as an incarnation and practised idolatry, (2) those who worshipped God under the name of Rāma, but rejected idolatry and the doctrine of incarnation, and (3) those who worshipped Kṛishṇa. In each group during this period Hindī literature came to be used and was one of the great factors which helped to spread the various movements, while they on the other hand helped to stimulate the growth of Hindī literature. Almost the whole of subsequent Hindi literature is impressed with one or another of these forms of Vaishṇava doctrine.

Malik Muhammad Jayasi.—The bardic chronicles had a much more local currency than the religious verse described above, and outside Rajputana contributed little to the development of vernacular literature, but one remarkable poem of this period seems to show how even the poetry of the bards had been affected by the religious revival. This was the *Padumāvatī* of *Malik Muhammad Jāyasī* who flourished about 1540. Malik Muhammad was a Muhammadan devotee, but was acquainted with Hindu lore, and profoundly affected by the teaching of Kabīr. He was much honoured by the Rājā of Ameṭhī, who attributed the birth of a son to the prayers of the saint, and his tomb is still to be seen at Ameṭhī. Besides the *Padumāvatī*, he wrote also a religious poem called the *Akharāvat*. In the *Padumāvatī* he tells the story of a certain Ratan Sen who, hearing from a parrot of the great beauty of Padumāvati, or Padminī, journeyed to Ceylon as a mendicant and returned to Chitor with Padminī as his bride. Alā-ud-dīn, the ruling sovereign at Delhi, also heard of Padminī and endeavoured to capture Chitor in order to gain possession of her. He was unsuccessful, but Ratan Sen was taken prisoner and held as a hostage for her surrender. He was afterwards released from captivity by the bravery of two heroes. He then attacked king Dev Pāl, who had made insulting proposals to Padminī during his imprisonment. Dev Pāl was killed, but Ratan Sen, who was mortally wounded, returned to Chitor only to die. His two wives, Padminī and another, became *satī* for him, and while this was happening Alā-ud-dīn appeared at the gates of Chitor, and though it was bravely defended, captured it. At the end of the poem Malik Muhammad explains it all as being an allegory. Chitor is the body of man, Ratan Sen is the soul, Padminī is wisdom, Alā-ud-dīn is delusion, the parrot is the *guru*, and so on, and thus a religious character is given to the story. Malik Muhammad's poem is based on the facts connected with the actual siege of Chitor, which took place in 1303, but he has considerably modified the details and borrowed also from other stories. The poem is written in the vernacular dialect of Malik Muhammad's time tinged slightly with an admixture of Persian words and idioms. It was originally written in the Persian character. It is a work of great originality and poetic beauty, and must be reckoned as one of the masterpieces of Hindī literature.

The following translation of an extract from Malik Muhammad's description of Ceylon will give some idea of his excellence as a poet:—

"When a man approacheth this land, 'tis as though he approacheth Kailāsa the mount of heaven. Dense mango-groves lie on every side, rising from the earth to the very sky. Each tall tree exhaleth the odours of mount Malaya, and the shade covereth the world as though it were the night. The shade is pleasant with its Malaya breeze; e'en in the fiery month of Jyeṣṭha [May-June] 'tis cool amidst it. It is as though night cometh from that shade and as though from it cometh the greenness of the sky. When the wayfarer cometh thither suffering from the heat he forgetteth his trouble in his blissful rest, and whoso hath found this perfect shade, returneth ne'er again to bear the sun-rays.

"So many and so dense are these groves, that I cannot tell their end. The whole six seasons of the year do they flower and fruit, as though it were always spring.

"The pleasant thick mango-groves bear fruit, and the more fruit they bear, the more (humbly) do the trees bow their heads. On the main branches and trunks of the jack trees, the jack fruit ripen, and fair appeareth the *baṛhal* to him who looketh. The *khirnī* ripeneth sweet as molasses, and the black wild plum, like black bees (among its leaves). Cocoanuts ripen and ripeneth the *khurhur;* they ripen as though the orchards were in Indra's heaven. From the *mahuā* doth such sweetness exude, that honey is its flavour, and flowers its scent; and in these princes' gardens are other good fruits, good to eat, whose names I knew not. They all appear with nectar-like branches, and he who once tasteth them remaineth ever longing for more.

"Areca and nutmeg, all fruits, are produced there luxuriantly. On every side are thick groves of tamarinds, of palmyras, and of date-palms.

"There dwell the birds, singing in many tongues, and sporting joyfully as they look upon these nectar-branches. At dawn the honey-suckers are fragrant, and the turtle-dove cries out ' 'Tis thou and only thou ' (*eka-i tū hī*). The emerald parroquets sportively rejoice, and the rock-pigeons cry *kurkur* and fly about. The hawk-cuckoo crieth for its beloved, and the skulking warbler shouted *tūhīṅ khī*. *Kuhū kuhū* ever crieth the cuckoo, while the king-crow speaketh in many tongues. 'Tyre, tyre' [*dahī, dahī*] crieth the milkmaid-bird, while the green pigeon plaintively telleth its tale of woe. The peacock's cry *kūṅ kūṅ* sounded sweet to the ear, and loudly caw the crows.

"Filling the orchards, sitteth every bird that hath a name, and each praiseth the Creator in his own tongue."[1]

Other Poets of this Period.—Two other poets of this period may also be mentioned—*Narottam Dās* (fl. 1530) wrote the *Sudāmā Charitr* and the *Dhruv Charitr*. These works are stories in verse. He was also the author of detached poems.

Kripā Rām (fl. 1540) was the author of a work entitled *Hit Taraṅgiṇī* written in Braj Bhāshā. Its importance lies in its being the earliest extant work in Hindī dealing with the art of poetry, and it shows how the way was being prepared for the work of Keśav Dās.

[1] *Padumāvatī*, Canto II. 27-29; Translation by Sir George A. Grierson and Pandit Sudhākara Dwivedi in *Bibliotheca Indica* of Asiatic Society of Bengal; New Series, No. 877, Vol. I. 15, 16.

V.

THE MUGHAL COURT AND THE ARTISTIC INFLUENCE IN HINDĪ LITERATURE

(1550-1800)

The New Influence in Hindi Poetry.—Although the religious language of the Muhammadans was Arabic, the literary language they used in India, and the language of the court, was Persian. This language possessed a large literature, which had already developed a highly artistic character before the Muhammadan power was established in India. Many Hindus who were connected with the court came to learn this language, and when Urdu literature developed it was fashioned after Persian models. Though Hindī developed on its own lines, without any direct influence from Persian, it seems not unlikely that the polished Persian verse with which many Hindus became acquainted may have suggested a higher artistic standard in Hindī literature than there had been before. At all events about the middle of the sixteenth century there appeared a new artistic influence in Hindī literature, which was developed under encouragement from the Mughal court.

Previous Muhammadan rulers had encourged literature, but it was Akbar who first extended patronage to those who wrote in Hindī. The reign of Akbar (1556-1605) was marked by its brilliance and splendour. Not only was he successful in war and in establishing a strong and, on the whole, good government, but he was also a great patron of art and literature. Architecture, music, painting and calligraphy were all encouraged. The Emperor established a large library of books of various languages, and had translations made from Sanskrit into Persian and the vernacular. Poets were patronized and rewarded with great liberality. The magnificence of such a reign, like the glorious reign of Queen Elizabeth in England which was contemporary with it, could not but exercise a stimulating influence on all sides, and this was felt in Hindī literature as well as in other directions. Even those writers who lived far away from the influence of the court were helped by feeling that they could carry on their labours in peace under a government strong enough to secure good order, and tolerant towards Hindus as well as Muhammadans. Akbar pursued a deliberate policy of protection and encouragement of Hindu learning. The patronage extended by him, and others in high position, to Hindu as well as to Muhammadan writers, stimulated a great outburst of literary activity, and encouraged improvement in the standards of poetic art. The influence was of course felt most by those writers who lived in close touch with the court.

Poets at Akbar's Court.—*Akbar* himself is the reputed author of a few detached verses in Hindī, in which he signs himself Akabbar Rāy. They were probably composed in the Emperor's name by the court musician Tān Sen. Some of Akbar's great ministers of state were also authors. It was largely due to the influence of Rājā *Ṭoḍar Mal* (1523-1589) in making Hindus learn Persian that Urdu was developed and accepted as a language. Besides translating the *Bhāgavata Purāṇa* into Persian, Ṭoḍar Mal was the author of some Hindī verses, the best being on morals (*nīti*). Rājā *Bīrbal* (1528-1583) was a Kanauji Dube Brahman, and was at first a poet at the court of the Rājā of Jaipur. The latter sent him to the court of Akbar, where his ability soon brought him into favour. He was not only skilled in business so that he soon rose to a high position, but also possessed great musical and poetical talent. Akbar gave him the title of *Kavi Rāy* (poet-laureate) and he received rapid promotion. He was famous as a poet for his short verses of a witty and humorous character. No complete work by him has survived, but many verses ascribed to him are still current. When he reached a high position he himself became a patron of other poets. Rājā *Manohar Dās* (fl. 1577), another of Akbar's courtiers, was also a poet. Mahārāja *Mān Singh* (1535-1618) of Jaipur, one of Akbar's generals, was a great patron of literary men, and is reputed to have given as much as a lakh of rupees for a single verse. *Abul Faiz* (or *Faizī*) was brother of Abul Fazl, who wrote the *Āīn-i-Akbarī*. Both were friends of Akbar. Abul Faiz was not only a Persian poet but the author of many Hindī couplets.

The most skilled Hindī poet amongst Akbar's great ministers of state was *Abdul Rahīm Kḥānkḥānā* (1553-1627). He was the son of Bairām Kḥān through whose aid Akbar, in his youth, had been established on the throne. He was acquainted with Arabic, Persian, Sanskrit and Hindī, and besides being a poet himself was a great patron of poets, especially of Gaṅg Kavi. His Hindī verses, especially those on morals (*nīti*) are very much admired, and he was a poet of a high order. Amongst the several works he produced is the *Rahīm Sat Saī* in which some of his best poetry is found.

Tān Sen (fl. 1560-1610) of Gwalior, a Hindu convert to Islam, was the most celebrated musician at Akbar's court and indeed of his age. After service at other courts he was summoned by Akbar in 1563, and the first time he performed Akbar is said to have given him two lakhs of rupees. Besides being a singer he also wrote poems in Hindī. He lived on into the reign of Jahāngīr. Amongst his compositions are the *Saṅgīt Sār* and the *Rāg Mālā*. *Rām Dās* of Gopchal, the father of the great poet Sūr Dās, was another great singer of Akbar's court, regarded as second only to Tān Sen. Among other Hindī poets who attended Akbar's court were the two friends *Karnes* (or *Karan*) and *Narhari Sahāy*. The latter was given by Akbar the title of *Mahāpātr*, the Emperor saying that other bards were vessels of virtue *(Guṇ kā pātr)*, but that Narhari Sahāy was a great vessel *(Mahāpātr)*.

A more famous poet connected with Akbar's court was *Gaṅga Prasād*, who is more commonly known as *Gaṅg Kavi.* He lived probably from about 1533 to 1617. Very little is known of his life, and though he was very much honoured in his day only about thirty or thirty-five of his verses are still extant. On one occasion Abdul Rahīm Kḥānkḥānā, who was his special patron, is reported to have given him as much as thirty-six lakhs of rupees for a single verse. He is said to have excelled in the comic style and also in his description of battles.

The Art of Poetry.—Besides the many poets who were closely connected with the court, the reign of Akbar was the period when such great poets as Tulsī Dās and Sūr Dās flourished. These will be dealt with in later chapters in connection with the religious movements with which they were connected. But more closely in touch with the court was a movement to systematize the art of poetry itself. While great writers like Tulsī Dās and Sūr Dās were far beyond their contemporaries in the success they achieved in the handling of metres and the polish of their verse, earlier poets had often failed in this respect. But the artistic influence which had been brought to bear on Hindī poetry now became self-conscious in various works, themselves in verse, which determined the canons of poetic criticism.

Kesav Das.—Kripā Rām, who is mentioned in a previous chapter, was probably the forerunner of this movement, but the first great writer on the art of poetry was *Keśav Dās Sanāḍhya Miśra* (1555-1617) of Oṛchhā in Bundelkhaṇḍ. His first important work was the *Vigyān Gītā*, which he dedicated to his patron Rājā Madhukar Shāh of Oṛchhā. His most admired work is his *Kavi Priyā*, in which he describes the various literary qualities which should mark a good poem and other matters connected with the art of poetry. This work, which has made Keśav Dās an authority on poetry, was dedicated to a famous courtesan of those days named *Pravin Rāy Pāturī*, who was also the authoress of numerous short poems which have a great reputation. The *Rām Chandrikā* of Keśav Dās was inscribed to Indrajīt Singh, son of Madhukar Shāh. It was Keśav Dās who, through Rājā Bīrbal's instrumentality, got Akbar to excuse Indrajīt from a heavy fine he had imposed upon him, and Keśav Dās was greatly honoured by Indrajīt. Keśav also wrote the learned *Rasik Priyā* on poetical composition (*sāhitya*) and the *Rām Alaṅkṛitmanjarī* on prosody. These works on poetry and kindred subjects were not only concerned with giving rules, but also provided original illustrations, so that each work is also a collection of verse of great poetic merit. The poetry of Keśav Dās is not easy reading, but there is no doubt of his being a poet of very great skill, and his name is to be reckoned amongst the foremost. Very many commentaries on his principal works have been written, and he has had many imitators. The translation of a few of his lines, which is all that we have space for here, can give only a very inadequate idea of his poetry:—

Keśav says my [grey] hairs have done to me what my enemies cannot do;
Maidens with a countenance fair as the moon, and eyes like deer, now call me Bābā [father].

* * * * *

Do not employ a Brahman who is greedy of fees; do not make a fool your friend ;
Do not serve an ungrateful master ; do not praise poetry that is full of defects.

* * * * *

Keśav says, When I see glancing eyes my good resolutions go, and the opinion of the world is no longer heeded ;
My ears become deaf to instruction, and my eyes closed to all discernment of right and wrong ;
The chariot-like motion of the good intentions of my mind becomes stopped like a river that has ceased to flow.
May the Creator forbid that such a woman should fix her eyes on me.

* * * * *

Avoid a horse with an unsteady gait, a servant who is a thief, a mind which is fickle, a friend without intelligence, a master who is a miser.

Taking food in another's house, dwelling in dog-kennels, travelling in the rainy season—these things, says Keśav Dās, give a lot of trouble.
Keeping company with sinners, a woman under the control of Cupid, a son of ill-fame—these are hurtful to the mind.
Folly, old age, sickness, poverty, falsehood, anxiety—these things, says Keśav, are a hell upon earth.

Some Contemporaries of Kesav Das.—The brother of Keśav Dās, whose name was *Balbhadra Sanāḍhya Miśra*, wrote several works which include a commentary on the *Bhāgavata Purāṇa*. His most famous poem is a *Nakhśikh*, which is recognized as a standard work. This is a form of literature which is common amongst Hindī writers, and is closely connected with works on the art of poetry. In a *Nakhśikh* every part of the body of a hero or heroine from the toe-nail *(nakh)* to the top-knot of the hair *(śikh)* is described with illustrative verses. Such a work was intended to be used by other poets in want of ideas. A similar kind of work is a work on lovers, or a *Nāyak-Nāyikā Bhed*, in which various kinds of heroes and heroines are described and classified with a minuteness which is often pedantic and absurd. Other writers on the art of poetry of this period were *Bāl Kṛishṇa Tripāṭhī* (fl. 1600) and *Kāśī Nāth* (fl. 1600), the former of whom wrote a good prosody called *Ras Chandrikā*.

Artistic Poets of the time of Jahangir and Shah Jahan.—The effects of the encouragement given to Hindī literature by Akbar lasted long after his death. Jahāngīr (1605-1627) and Shāh Jahān (1627-1658) very largely continued Akbar's policy of encouraging poets. Dārā Shukoh, the son of Shāh Jahān, was a great patron of learning and literature with a strong leaning towards Hinduism. Even in the time of Aurangzeb (1658-1707), although he was unfavourable to Hindu learning, the title of *Kavi Rāy* continued to be given to deserving poets.

Sundar (fl. 1631) was a Brahman who held the title of *Kavi Rāy* at the court of Shāh Jahān. He wrote a work on poetical composition called *Sundar Sṛiṅgār*, and was also the author of a Braj Bhāshā version of the *Singhāsan Battīsī*, which was afterwards translated into Urdu by Lallū Jī Lāl.

Senāpati was born about 1589 and died after 1649. He was a Kanaujī Brahman and a devotee of Kṛishṇa. His principal work was the *Kavitta Ratnākar*, which is dated 1649, and deals with various aspects of the art of poetry as well as other matters. He excelled in his description of nature, and is especially famous for his description of the six seasons in which he is considered to have excelled all Hindī poets with the exception of Dev Datt. Another work of his is the *Kāvya Kalpadrum*. His poems were probably written as detached verses and collected afterwards. The following is from his description of spring (*basant*):—

"During the sportive spring the *palās* trees are in full bloom, with red flowers, parts of which however appear from their blackness to have been dipped in ink. Swarms of bees are going to them to gather honey. The mild south wind is blowing fragrance in the gardens and forests. The poet Senāpati says, 'In the spring, by constantly looking at these flowers the idea of writing poetry has been strongly brought to my mind.' The red glow of the upper part of the flowers clearly pourtrays the burning desire and yearning of a lover, while the blackness of the lower part, like a fire burnt out completely and turned to charcoal, suggests the pangs of separation."

The Tripathi Brothers.—Ratnākar Tripāṭhī was a Kanaujī Brahman who lived at Tikvāmpur in the district of Cawnpore and had four sons, all of whom became famous Hindī poets. They flourished in the reigns of Shāh Jahān and Aurangzeb in the latter half of the seventeenth century and amplified and developed the work of Keśav Dās. The eldest was *Chintāmaṇi Tripāṭhī*, who was patronised by several rulers as well as by the Emperor Shāh Jahān. He is regarded as one of the great authorities on the subject of poetical composition (*sāhitya*). Among his works are *Chhand Bichār*, a treatise on prosody, *Kāvya Vivek*, *Kavi-kul Kalpataru*, and *Kāvya Prakāś*. He was also the author of a *Rāmāyaṇ* in *kavitta* and other metres. The name of the youngest brother was Jaṭā Śankar or *Nīl Kaṇṭh Tripāṭhī*. Both Chintāmaṇi and Nīl

Kaṇṭh were excelled as poets by the other two brothers, Bhūshaṇ and Mati Rām.

Bhūshaṇ Tripāṭhī visited the courts of several kings, but his special patrons were Śiv Rāj (or Śivājī) of Sitāra and Chhatrasāl of Pannā. On one occasion the latter monarch helped with his own shoulder to carry the poet's palanquin, and Śiv Rāj bestowed lavish rewards upon him, giving on one occasion five elephants and twenty-five thousand rupees for a single poem. The principal work of Bhūshaṇ is the *Śiv Rāj Bhūshaṇ* which is an excellent account of rhetoric as used in poetry, and each figure of rhetoric is illustrated by a verse in honour of Śiv Rāj. It was composed between 1666 and 1673. Some of the works of Bhūshaṇ have been lost. But besides the *Śiv Rāj Bhūshaṇ* there are extant other verses in praise of Śiv Rāj and of Chhatrasāl. Bhūshaṇ is considered to have excelled in the tragic, heroic, and terrible styles, and holds a very high rank amongst Hindī poets. He is especially famous for his keen interest in the progress and glory of the Hindus, and this is one of the features of his poetry which is very much admired. It was this interest which attached him so much to Śivājī, the Marāṭhā hero, who did so much to weaken the Muhammadan power. Here is a translation of one of his verses :—

> "As Indra subdued Jambha, as the *bāṛav* fire overcomes the sea, as Rāmachandra overcame the hypocrite Rāvan, as the wind overpowers the waters, as Śambhu overcame Cupid, as Rāma, the Lord of Brahmans, overcame Sahasra Bāl, as fire overcomes the branches of a tree, as a leopard overcomes a herd of deer, as a lion overcomes elephants, as light overcomes darkness, as Kṛishṇa overcame Kānha, so, Bhushaṇ says, the lion Śiv Rāj overcomes the Muhammadans."

Mati Rām Tripāṭhī lived first at the court of Mahārāja Rāv Bhāū Singh of Būndī and afterwards at that of Rājā Śambhu Nāth Sulānkī. In honour of his first patron he composed a work on rhetoric called *Lalit Lalām*. Among the illustrative verses are many in praise of his patron as well as love verses and others. His work is considered to give a very clear and easily understood account of the subject of rhetoric. It was composed about 1664. The *Chhand Sār Pingal* is a treatise on prosody composed in honour of Śambhu Nāth. The *Ras Rāj* is a treatise on lovers containing a *Nāyikā Bhed* and is considered to be a very excellent work. Mati Rām also composed the *Sat Saī Mati Rām*. As a poet he is famed for the purity and sweetness of his language, the excellence of his similes, and for his descriptions of the dispositions of men. Many of his *dohās* are considered equal to those of Bihārī Lāl.

Other Poets of the time of Shah Jahan.—Rājā Śambhu Nāth Singh of Sitārā (fl. 1650) was the friend and patron of Mati Rām and other poets. He was the author of a *Nāyikā Bhed* and a *Nakhśikh* which are much admired. The latter is sometimes considered to be the best work of its kind extant.

Sarasvatī (fl. 1650) was a Brahman of Benares, learned in Sanskrit composition. At the instance of Shāh Jahān he took to writing poems in Hindī. His chief work of this kind was the *Kavindrā Kalpa Latā*, in which there are many poems in praise of his patron as well as of prince Dārā Shukoh and the Begam Sāhibā.

Tulsī (fl. 1655) was only a mediocre poet himself, but in 1655 he compiled an excellent anthology of poetry, called the *Kavi Mālā*, which includes poems by seventy-five different authors from 1443 to 1643.

Another writer of this period was *Vedāng Rāy* (fl. circ. 1650). He was the author of the *Pārsī Prakāś*, a work describing the manner of counting the months, etc., by Hindus and Muhammadans, which was compiled by the orders of the Emperor Shāh Jahān.

Bihari Lal Chaube.—The most celebrated Hindī writer in connection with the art of poetry is *Bihārī Lāl Chaube* (circ. 1603-1663). He is said to have been born in Gwalior and to have spent his boyhood in Bundelkhaṇḍ. On his marriage he settled at Muttra the home of the Braj Bhāshā dialect, in which his verses are composed. His patron was Rājā Jai Singh of Jaipūr, who gave him a gold *ashrafī* for each *dohā*. Bihārī Lāl's fame as a poet rests upon his *Sat Saī*

(1662), which is a collection of approximately seven hundred *dohās* and *sorațhās*. The majority of the couplets take the shape of amorous utterances of Rādhā and Kṛishṇa, but each couplet is complete in itself. They are intended to illustrate figures of rhetoric and other constituents of a poem. As the verses do not connect themselves into a story the order of their arrangement can be changed and they have come down in different recensions. The most famous is that made for prince Āzam Shāh, the third son of the Emperor Aurangzeb, and hence called the Āzam Shāhī recension. A brief description of this work will help to indicate the nature of Hindī works on poetics. The vast amount of literature of this type seems to indicate that in India the dictum that a poet is born and not made would have to be reversed. In the Āzam Shāhī recension there are first a few miscellaneous verses. Then there are verses applicable to each of four kinds of hero (*nāyak*), followed by nearly two hundred verses which describe the varieties and sub-varieties of heroine (*nāyikā*). Next there are verses illustrating the various constituents of poetic style (*ras*), its excitants and its ensuants, among which verses about a hundred and seventy deal with the pangs of love in separation. The third section is a *Nakhśikh*, and ends with verses descriptive of the six Indian seasons. In the fourth part there are moral apophthegms and allusive sayings and a collection of verses illustrating sentiments appropriate to various occasions. In the last part besides the conclusion and other verses there are verses illustrating the different styles (*ras*) of poetry, which are considered in India to be nine in number. These are *hāsya* (comic), *karuṇā* (pathetic), *raudra* (furious), *vīra* (heroic), *bhayānaka* (terrible), *bibhatsa* (disgustful), *adbhuta* (marvellous), *śānta* (quietistic), and *sṛingāra* (erotic). Only the first eight are referred to in this part of the *Sat Saī*, as the last (*sṛingāra*) had already been dealt with at length in an earlier part of the recension.

Bihāri Lāl was not the originator of this form of composition. Similar works had appeared in Sanskrit, one of which is called *Sapta Satikā*, the Sanskrit equivalent of the Hindī *Sat Saī* ("seven centuries," *i.e.* of verse). Tulsī Dās had written a *Sat Saī* before the time of Bihārī Lāl, as well as other Hindī poets. But Bihārī Lāl undoubtedly achieved very great excellence in this particular line, and his work has had a large number of commentators (as many as thirty in number) and many imitators. Hari Prasād (fl. circ. 1775) of Benares translated the *Sat Saī* into Sanskrit. Each couplet had to be complete in itself, and yet in such a small space the poet must give an entire picture. Conciseness of style was therefore an absolute necessity, and besides this all the different artifices of Indian rhetoric had to be illustrated in turn. The work of Bihāri Lāl is a triumph of skill and of felicity in expression. He is perhaps at his best in his description of natural phenomena, as when he describes the scent-laden breeze under the guise of a way-worn pilgrim from the south. Naturally a work of this kind abounds in obscurities and on account of the peculiarity of its style is very difficult to translate. In the following verse Bihārī Lāl gives a riddle:—

At even came the rogue, and with my tresses
  Toyed with a sweet audace—with ne'er a 'please'
Snatched a rude kiss—then wooed me with caresses.
  'Who was it, dear ?' 'Thy love ?' 'No, dear, the breeze.'[1]

Jaswant Singh.—*Mahārāja Jaswant Singh* of Jodhpur (Māṛwār) figures in history as an opponent of Aurangzeb. He was born in 1625 and died in 1681. In 1634, while still a boy, he came to the throne. In literature his chief fame rests on his *Bhāshā Bhūshaṇ*, a work on rhetoric in 261 *dohās*. This work, which was founded on a Sanskrit one, has had a large number of commentators. Though Keśav Dās was the first great Hindī writer on this subject he is considered heretical in some points, and for those who do not follow Keśav

[1] Translation from *Imperial Gazetteer of India*, Vol. II, p. 423.

Dās, the *Bhāshā Bhūshaṇ* is the great text-book. Jaswant Singh was the author of several other poems which are connected with the Vedānta philosophy.

Dev Kavi.—*Dev Datt*, more commonly known as *Dev Kavi* (circ. 1673-1745) was a Sanāḍhya Brahman who was born at Etawah. At the age of sixteen he recited his first effort before Prince Āzam Shāh. In search of a patron he visited many places in India but seems to have been dissatisfied with each in turn. His most famous patron was Rājā Bhogī Lāl. His various wanderings enabled him to give accurate descriptions of the inhabitants of different parts of India. He was a prolific writer and is credited by some with having composed as many as seventy-two different works. Only about thirty of these are extant. They include a play called *Dev Māyā Prapañch* and works on the art. of poetry. Amongst his most famous works are the *Jātibilās*, the *Rasbilās*, and the *Premchandrikā*. Most of his verse is of an erotic character, but from the point of view of form and language he is to be reckoned amongst the greatest Hindī poets. He wrote in Braj Bhāshā, and his verse is adorned with all the recognised ornaments of style. In his handling of rhymes, his use of attributes, his drawing of comparisons, his knowledge of the sayings current amongst men, and his description of heroines who represent women typical of various parts of India, he is considered to have shown the greatest skill.

Here are some translations of his verses :—

"Call me a wicked person, noble or ignoble, call me poor, or one who is to be blamed, call me a woman of ill-fame—whether in this world, the world of men, or in the best of worlds I dwell, nevertheless I am separate from all these worlds ; whether my body is destroyed, or the gods and gurus are destroyed, or my life is destroyed, I will not give up my obstinacy. He who dwells in Brindāban, wearing a crown and yellow garments, with him I am madly in love."

* * * * *

"The work of a man of noble race, the gentility of a nobleman, the wealth of a generous man, a woman of good character, the honour of giving, generosity like that of Sūr Dās, the lustre of virtue, a woman who walks like an elephant, water in the hot weather, the sunshine of October, the smiling lightning accompanied by clouds during the

month of November, the full moon, the morning sun, the days of the winter season, the nights of spring—Dev says these are most excellent."

Later Writers on the Art of Poetry.—The reign of Aurangzeb (1658-1707) was marked by the beginning of the decay of the Mughal Empire. It was also the time when a period of decadence in Hindī poetry set in. This however was not felt at first as is shown by the names mentioned above. But towards the end of Aurangzeb's reign, and still more after his time in the eighteenth century, the decline becomes evident. While the number of poets still continues to be great there are no names of such outstanding importance as marked the time of Akbar and his immediate successors, and most of the writers are only imitators of greater poets who preceded them. The severe Aurangzeb was unfavourable to the arts and to Hindu learning, but the court patronage of poets was not entirely withdrawn, and many poets attended his court and also that of his son Bahādur Shāh (1707-1712). The following are some of the writers on the art of poetry and kindred subjects from the time of Aurangzeb down to the end of the eighteenth century:—

Kulpati Miśra (born circ. 1620) was a Chaube Brahman of Agra and a nephew of Bihārī Lāl Chaube. He attended the court of Mahārāja Rām Singh of Jaipūr. His chief work, which is dated 1670, is the *Ras Rahasya*, a work on poetics.

Rām Jī (born 1646) was the author of a *Nāyikā Bhed* as well as other works.

Maṇḍan (born 1643), of Bundelkhaṇḍ, wrote several works on poetical composition.

Sukh Dev Miśra (fl. circ. 1680), of Kampilā, attended several courts. The Rājā of Gauṛ gave him the title of *Kavirāj*. He wrote works on prosody, poetical composition and other subjects and is considered a poet of very great merit.

Newāj (fl. circ. 1700) was a Brahman who lived at the Court of Rājā Chhatrasāl of Pannā. He was the author of a play called the *Śakuntalā Nāṭak* as well as of many detached verses.

Kālidās Trivedī (fl. circ. 1700), of Banpurā in the Doab, was for many years in attendance at the court of Aurangzeb, and afterwards at that of the Rājā of Jambū. He is considered to be an excellent poet. Among other works he compiled an anthology, called *Kālidās Hajārā*, which contains a thousand poems selected from the works of over two hundred poets from 1423 to 1718.

Ālam (fl. 1703) was a Brahman who fell in love with a Muhammadan woman named Shekh Rangrezin, who was a dyer by trade. He became a Muhammadan and married her. *Shekh Rangrezin* also wrote poetry. Ālam was in the service of Muazzam Shāh, son of Aurangzeb. His poetry is considered to be very beautiful.

Śrīpati (fl. 1720) is counted as one of the authorities on poetical composition. His most famous work is the *Kāvya Saroj*. He wrote several other works also.

Sūrati Miśra (fl. 1729), of Agra, wrote a commentary on the *Sat Saī* of Bihāri Lāl, and also one on the *Rasik Priyā* of *Keśāv Dās*. He also wrote works on rhetoric and other subjects, including a *Nakhśikh*.

Gañjan (fl. 1729), of Benares, was a Brahman who was in the service of Qamruddīn Khān (the Vazīr of the Emperor Muhammad Shāh) who gave the poet liberal rewards. At the orders of his patron Ganjan wrote a work on poetics in which there are many verses in praise of the Vazīr. It is considered to be a work of great merit.

Guru Datt Singh (fl. 1734) was Rājā of Amethī. He wrote under the name of *Bhūpati*. His principal work was an excellent *Sat Saī* in imitation of that of Bihārī Lāl.

Tosh Nidhi (fl. 1734) lived at Singraur in the district of Allahabad. He wrote the *Sudhānidhi* and other works on poetics including a *Nakhśikh*, which are much admired.

Dalpati Rāy, a merchant, and *Bansidhar*, a Brahman (fl. 1735), both of whom lived at Ahmedabad, wrote in collaboration the *Alaṅkār Ratnākar*. It was inscribed to Rājā Jagat Singh, of Udaipur, and is a kind of commentary on the Bhāshā Bhūshaṇ of Rājā Jaswant Singh.

Somnāth (fl. 1737) was a Brahman who was patronised by a son of the Rājā of Bharatpur. Among other works he wrote the *Pīyūsh Nidhi*, which is considered to be a standard work on the art of poetry.

Ras Līn (fl. 1740), whose real name was Sayyad Gulām Nabī, of Bilgrām, in the district of Hardoī, wrote several works on poetics which include a *Nakhśikh* called *Aṅg Darpan.*

Uday Nāth Trivedī (fl. 1740), of Banpurā in the Doab, was the son of Kālidās Trivedī. He was the poet-laureate at the court of the Rājā of Ameṭhī, and wrote on the subject of poetics. His son *Dūlah Trivedi* (fl. 1750) also wrote on the same subject.

Bairī Sāl (fl. 1768) wrote on the subject of rhetoric. His *Bhāshā Bharaṇ* is considered to be a standard work of great excellence.

Kishor (fl. 1768) was an excellent poet whose various detached verses are collected in the *Kishor Saṅgrah.* He is considered to be very successful in his description of the six seasons.

Datt or *Dev Datt* (fl. circ. 1770) was the author of the *Lālitya Latā*, a work on rhetoric which is said to resemble the *Lalit Lalām* of Mati Rām.

Chandan Rāy (fl. 1773) attended the court of the Rājā of Gaur. He wrote many esteemed works on the art of poetry. He had twelve pupils, all of whom became successful poets.

Ratan Kavi (born circ. 1741) wrote works on poetics, which include the *Fateh Shāh Prakāś* and the *Fateh Bhūshaṇ.* He is considered to be a poet of great merit. His examples are mostly verses in praise of his patron Fateh Shāh of Bundelā.

Manī Rām Miśra (fl. 1772) has given in the fifty-six verses of his *Chhand Chhappani* a very concise and well-written account of the art of poetry. This poem, which somewhat resembles the Sanskrit Sutras, is considered to be very excellent.

Bodhā Fīrozābādī (fl. circ. 1773-1803) was connected with Pannā. He was the author of the *Ishqnāmā* and some detached verses which are much admired. He was a poet of love, and his verses were written mostly in praise of a courtesan named Subhān.

Jan Gopāl (fl. 1776) was the author of the *Samarsār*, a work which is said to be full of poetic feeling.

Devkī Nandan (fl. 1784-1800) wrote the *Sṛingār Charitr*, which is a *Nāyak-Nāyikā Bhed*, and other much-praised works connected with the art of poetry.

Thān Rām, or *Thān* (fl. 1791), a Bhāṭ, was the author of a work on poetics called *Dalel Prakāś*.

Benī (fl. 1792-1817) wrote works on poetics, rhetoric, etc. His best verses are said to be verses of satire.

Bhaun (fl. 1794), a Bhāṭ, who was skilled in all the graces of poetry, wrote in Braj Bhāshā works connected with the poetic art.

Bhikārī Dās (fl. 1734-1750) was a Kayasth of Pratāpgaṛh, in Bundelkhaṇḍ. He is more generally known by the name of *Dās*. His patron was Hindūpati, brother of Rājā Prithvīpati. He borrowed phrases from other poets, especially from Śrīpati, but is considered nevertheless to be an excellent poet. Besides many works connected with the art of poetry he also translated the *Vishṇu Purāṇa* into Hindī verse.

Gumān Miśra (fl. 1744) attended the court of Akbar Ali Khān. He translated the *Naishadha* of Śri Harsha and wrote several works on poetics.

Raghu Nāth (fl. 1745), of Benares, was the father of Gokul Nāth, who is celebrated as the translator of the *Mahābhārata* into Hindī. Raghu Nāth was a writer on the art of poetry, his works being much admired. They include a commentary on the Sat Saī of Bihārī Lāl.

Kumār Maṇi Bhaṭṭ (fl. 1746) was a very skilled poet, who wrote a good work on poetics called *Rasik Rasāl*.

Śambhu Nāth Miśra (fl. 1749) attended the court of Bhagwant Rāy Khīchī, Rājā of Asothar. He wrote several much-admired works on poetics and was the preceptor of Śiv Arselā and other poets.

Śiv Arselā (fl. circ. 1750) wrote on poetical composition and prosody.

Jagat Singh (fl. circ. 1770) belonged to the family of the Rājā of Goṇḍā and Bhingā and was a pupil of Śiv Arselā. He wrote on prosody and rhetoric.

Ṭhākur (fl. circ. 1750) excelled especially in the *savaiya* metre, and his works are mostly in the erotic style. His most famous work is the *Ṭhākur Śatak*. He also wrote a commentary on the *Sat Saī* of Bihārī Lāl.

Hari Charan Dās (fl. 1778) was a Brahman, of Kṛishṇagaṛh (Māṛwār). He wrote commentaries on the *Kavi Priyā* and *Rasik Priyā* of Keśav Dās, as well as on the *Sat Saī* of Bihārī Lāl, and was the author of other works also.

VI.

TULSĪ DĀS AND THE RĀMA CULT

(1550-1800)

Tulsi Das.—The most celebrated name in Hindī literature is undoubtedly that of *Tulsī Dās*, whose Hindī *Rāmāyaṇ* has had great and deserved fame not only in India but throughout the whole world. The details of his life, apart from legends, are very scanty. He is said to have been born about 1532, and his father's name is given as Ātma Rām and his mother's as Hulasī. His own name was at first Rāmbolā, but when he became a devotee he took the name of Tulsī Dās. The place of his birth is not known with certainty. According to some he was born at Hastināpur; according to others at Hājīpur, near Chitrakūṭ. But the tradition which is most generally accepted is that he was born at Rājpur, in the district of Bāndā. He was a Kanaujī Brahman, and it is said that his *guru* was Narharidās, who was sixth in preceptorial succession from Rāmānanda. He himself tells us, in the introduction to the *Rāmāyaṇ*, that he studied at Sūkar-khet, or Soron. When he was a young man it is said that he loved his wife very much, and one day, when she had gone home to her father's house, Tulsī Dās was greatly troubled on account of separation from her. He therefore hastened after her, although it involved crossing a swollen river in the dark. His wife, however, rebuked him, saying that if only he would have as great devotion to Rāma, the earth would become gold. These words acted as a call to Tulsī Dās. At daybreak he left home, and became a devotee of Rāma, taking up his abode at Benares.

There he spent the greater part of his life, though he also visited other places, such as Soron, Ayodhyā, Chitrakūṭ, Allahabad, and Brindāban. Many legends are told about him, but scarcely anything that is reliable. Nābhā Dās, the author of the *Bhaktamālā*, is said to have been his friend, and Sūr Dās is also supposed to have visited him. He was not directly connected with the court, though Rājā Mān Singh and Abdul Rahīm Khānkhānā are said to have befriended him, and no doubt he was affected by the artistic influence in literature which was characteristic of the age in which he lived. Tulsī Dās died at Benares in 1624.

The great masterpiece of Tulsī Dās is the *Rāmāyaṇ*. This is the name by which it is generally known, but he himself called it the *Rām-charit-mānas*, the "Lake of the deeds of Rāma." It was commenced in 1575, according to his own statement in the prologue. The story of Rāma had been told long before by the Sanskrit poet Vālmīki, who lived probably in the fourth century B.C., and it has been a frequent theme of Indian poets in the various languages of India. The *Rāmāyaṇ* of Tulsī Dās is not, however, a translation of that of his Sanskrit predecessor. The general outline of the story is the same, but there is a great deal of difference in treatment. It is only in the broadest outline that the two agree. Not only are there different episodes in each, but even in the main story the incidents are differently placed and often have quite a different complexion. The main difference, however, between the work of Vālmīki and that of Tulsī Dās is in their theological outlook. In books II to VI of Vālmīki's poem Rāma appears as a man and only a man, except in one passage which has been interpolated into the sixth book. The first book, in which Rāma and his brothers are regarded as partial incarnations of Vishṇu, is considered by scholars as a later addition. In the poem of Tulsī Dās, however, Rāma appears throughout as an incarnation of the Supreme God. The same theological position as that of Tulsī Dās was also characteristic of a Sanskrit work by an unknown poet called the *Adhyātma Rāmāyaṇ*, the date of which is not earlier than the fourteenth century A.D. It is not unlikely that it was this work which was the real precursor of Tulsī Dās's *Rāmāyaṇ*. Besides their theological attitude they have other points in common, but even a casual acquaintance with the two poems will make it clear that the work of Tulsī Dās is far superior in poetic merit.

Tulsī Dās was in line with that tendency of the *bhakti* movement, which we have already noted in a previous chapter, in using the vernacular for his great poem. But he knew he would meet with his critics, especially amongst the Sanskrit pandits, who would affect to despise his work as a concession to the uneducated multitude. There is quite a long passage in the introduction to the *Rāmāyaṇ* in which he vindicates his style against the critics. "My lot," he writes, "is low, my purpose high; but I am confident of one thing, that the good will be gratified to hear me though fools may laugh. The laughter of fools will be grateful to me—as they have no taste for poetry nor love for Rāma I am glad that they should laugh. If my homely speech and poor wit are fit subjects for laughter, let them laugh; it is no fault of mine. If they have no understanding of true devotion to the Lord, the tale will seem insipid enough; but to the true and orthodox worshippers of Hari and Hara the story of Raghubar will be sweet as honey." The wonderful acceptance, however, which the poem of Tulsī Dās has received has been its greatest vindication. Amongst all classes of the Hindu community in North India, with the exception perhaps of a few Sanskrit pandits, it is to-day everywhere appreciated and venerated whether by rich or poor, old or young, learned or unlearned, and it has sometimes been called the Bible of the Hindu people of North India.

One most commendable feature of the *Rāmāyaṇ* is its pure and lofty moral tone, in which it compares very favourably with the literature put forth by some of the devotees of Kṛishṇa. In one passage, in which Tulsī Dās has been explaining why he calls his poem the "Lake (or "pond") of Rāma's deeds," he says, "Sensual wretches are like the cranes and crows that have no part in such a pond nor ever come near it; for here are no prurient and seductive stories, like snails or frogs and scum on the water, and therefore the lustful crow and greedy crane, if they do come, are disappointed." This claim made by Tulsī Dās was a just one, and it is this feature of his poem which has given it so much value in holding up a high moral ideal before its readers.

The dialect which Tulsī Dās uses is the old Baiswārī, or Avadhī, dialect of Eastern Hindī, and through his influence Rāmaite poetry since his day has generally been in this dialect. He uses, however, many words from other dialects, especially from Braj Bhāshā. His language abounds in colloquialisms, and Tulsī Dās has little scruple in altering a word, or adopting a corrupt pronunciation, to make it fit into his metre or rhyme. Like other Indian poets he makes use of many conventional similes and stereotyped phrases. The gem which is supposed to be in the serpent's head, and the mythical power of the swan to separate milk from the water with which it has been mixed, and his constant use of such phrases as "lotus-feet," are examples. But there are many other passages which show that Tulsī Dās was a true observer and lover of nature. In one place he speaks of King Daśrath, in his great distress, writhing "like a fish in the scour of a turbid river," a passage which, Mr. Growse tells us, puzzled commentators until someone discovered that this was a true phenomenon of nature. Tulsī Dās's love of nature comes out in many such passages as the following, taken from the *Āraṇya Kāṇḍ*:—

"The Lord went on from there to the shore of the deep and beautiful lake called Pampā; its water as clear as the soul of the saints; with charming flights of steps on each of its four sides; where beasts of different kinds came as they listed, to drink of the flood, like crowds of beggars at a good man's gate. Under its cover of dense lotus-leaves the water was as difficult to distinguish as is the unembodied supreme spirit under the veil of delusive phenomena. The happy fish were all in placid repose at the bottom of the deep pool, like the days of the righteous that are passed in peace. Lotuses of many colours displayed their flowers; there was a buzzing of garrulous bees, both honeymakers and bumble-bees; while swans and waterfowl were so noisy you would think they had recognised the Lord and were telling his praises. The geese and cranes and other birds were so numerous that only seeing would be believing, no words could describe them. The delightful voice of so many beautiful birds seemed as an invitation to the wayfarers. The saints had built themselves a house near the lake, with magnificent forest-trees all round—the *champa*, the *mālsari*, the *kadamb* and *tamāla*, the *pātala*, the *kathal*, the *dhāk* and the mango. Every tree had put forth its new leaves and flowers and was resonant with swarms of bees. A delightful air, soft, cool and fragrant, was ever in delicious motion, and the cooing of the cuckoos was so pleasant to hear that a saint's meditation would be broken by it. The trees, laden with fruits, bowed low to the ground, like a generous soul whom every increase of fortune renders only more humble than before."[1]

The story is divided into seven chapters, or *kāṇḍs*, named respectively *Bāl*, *Ayodhyā*, *Āraṇya*, *Kishkindhā*, *Sundar*, *Lankā*, and *Uttara*. Of these the second, which describes the scenes at Ayodhyā that led up to Rāma's banishment to the forest, is considered the best. The characters are consistently drawn, and many of the scenes are full of deep pathos. The grief of Daśrath, the filial piety meekness, generosity and nobility of Rāma, the wifely devotion of Sītā, the courage and enthusiasm of Lakshman, the unselfishness of Bharat, as the genius of Tulsī Dās has described them, cannot but awaken a response in the heart of the reader.

The object which Tulsī Dās had in mind, however, was not merely to tell in beautiful verse a wonderful story, but to use it as a vehicle for preaching the supreme value of the worship of Rāma. Though Tulsī Dās accepted, like other leaders of the Vaishṇava movement, the pantheistic teaching of the Vedānta, it was tempered by belief in a personal God, whom he identified with the incarnation Rāma. His poem is a passionate appeal to men to devote themselves to the worship of this God. The theological digressions

[1] Translation by Mr. F. S. Growse.

which Tulsī Dās sometimes makes, and the frequent hymns he inserts, may be to some extent a drawback to the literary value of the *Rāmāyaṇ*, but they are excused by the purpose which Tulsī Dās had in view. In these hymns the powers of Tulsī Dās as a poet are manifest, and even those who do not accept his religious ideas cannot but admire the spiritual earnestness which the hymns display. The following is from the *Bāl Kāṇḍ*:—

"To the King of heaven be all glory given, refuge of creation in distress and care,
Priests and kine befriending, hell's brief triumph ending, best beloved of Lakshmi, Ocean's daughter fair.
Heaven and earth's upholder, who, than all men bolder, dares to scan the secret of thy strange mysterious way?
Ever kind and loving, humble souls approving, may thy gracious favour reach now to me, I pray.
Spirit all-pervading, fleshly sense evading, hail Mukund immortal, lord of blissfulness supreme.
Ever pure and hōly, whom the Queen of Folly has no power to tangle in her world-deluding dream.
Glory, glory, glory, theme of endless story, sung by saints and sages in an ecstasy of love.
Daily, nightly gazing on the sight amazing, source of every blessing, Hari, lord of heaven above.
Triune incarnation, who at earth's creation, wert alone presiding, and other aid was none;
Though in prayer unable, and my faith unstable, O great sin-destroyer, hear our hapless moan.
Life's alarms dispelling, all disasters quelling, comfort of the faithful, be our succour now;
All the gods implore thee, falling low before thee, with unfeigned submission of body, soul, and vow.
Lord God Bhagavāna, Ved and eke Purāṇa, Sāradā and Seshnāg, and all the saintly throng,
Find the theme too spacious, only know thee gracious; hasten then to help us in our hour of wrong.
In all grace excelling, Beauty's chosen dwelling, ark on life's dark ocean, home of all most sweet,
God and saints and sages, now this tempest rages, fly in consternation to clasp thy lotus feet."[1]

The *Rāmāyaṇ* is undoubtedly a great poem, worthy to rank amongst the great classical masterpieces of the world's literature. It is not indeed without its literary

[1] Translation by Mr. F. S. Growse.

defects, and other Hindī poets, such as Sūr Dās, may have excelled Tulsī Dās in the polish of their verse and their handling of metres. But the *Rāmāyaṇ* of Tulsī Dās will always hold its place as the work of a great literary genius. The importance of its influence, too, cannot be exaggerated. Tulsī Dās founded no sect, and indeed added nothing to the theology of that school of Hinduism to which he belonged, but there is no doubt that the *Rāmāyaṇ* has been the most potent factor in making Vaishṇavism the accepted cult of the vast majority of Hindus in North India to-day.

A brief mention must be made of the other literary works of Tulsī Dās. All of them have the object of popularizing the worship of Rāma. In the *Rām Gītāvalī* Tulsī Dās tells the story of Rāma in verses which are adapted for singing. The *Dohāvalī*, or *Dohā Rāmāyaṇ*, is a collection of *dohās* and is not so much an epic poem as a moral work. Sir George Grierson thinks that it is probably a collection of *dohās* from other poems of Tulsī Dās, made by a later hand. The *Kavittāvalī*, or *Kavittsambandh*, also deals with the story of Rāma and is written in *kavitta* metre. The *Vinay Patrikā* is a collection of hymns to Rāma and is a work which is very much admired. The *Sat Saī* is a similar work to that which Bihārī Lāl wrote fifty years later, but is connected with Rāma instead of with Kṛishṇa. It contains seven hundred emblematic *dohās*. It is dated 1585. A great many other works also are ascribed to Tulsī Dās, but with regard to the genuineness of some of them there is a great deal of doubt. Although the *Rām-charit-mānas* is undoubtedly his greatest work his poetic powers are also exhibited in the other works which he composed.

The Bhaktamala.—It marks the greatness of the achievement of Tulsī Dās that amongst Rāmānandīs, or other worshippers of Rāma as the incarnation of the Supreme, there seem to be fewer Hindī works of outstanding importance than in other sections of the Vaishṇava movement, and this is no doubt due to the dominating influence of Tulsī Dās's great work. There are, however, some writers who must be mentioned. The *Bhaktamālā* was the work of *Nābhā Dās* (fl. 1600), who was also known as *Nārāyaṇ Dās.* He was the disciple of Agra Dās, who according to some was a leader of the Vallabha movement of Kṛishṇa worship, but by others is said to have been a disciple of Rāmānanda. Nābhā Dās was a Dom by caste, and it is said that when he was a child he was exposed by his parents during a time of famine to perish in the woods. Agra Dās found him and brought him up. It was at the suggestion of his preceptor that Nābhā Dās, when he arrived at maturity, wrote the *Bhaktamālā*, probably somewhere between 1585 and 1623. The *Bhaktamālā*, or "Roll of the Bhagats," is a poem in old Western Hindī, written mainly in the *chhappai* metre. It gives an account of the principal Vaishṇava devotees, whether worshippers of Rāma or of Kṛishṇa, though it deals chiefly with those who were worshippers of Rāma. Nābhā Dās himself seems to have been a Rāmānandī. The style is very obscure and compressed. Generally one stanza only is given to each devotee, and in this his chief characteristics are described in the briefest possible manner, with allusions to different legendary events in his life. The *Bhaktamālā* holds a very important place in Indian religious history. It would, however, be almost unintelligible but for the commentary which always accompanies it. This was written in the *kavitta* metre by *Priyā Dās* in 1712. In this commentary further legends are added. There have also been other later commentators, and their work is often printed together with the original text of *Nābhā Dās* and the gloss of *Priyā Dās.* The *Bhaktamālā* has been fully translated and adapted in all the chief vernaculars of India.

Maluk Das.—*Malūk Dās*, who lived in the reign of Aurangzeb, was the founder of a sect which is closely connected with the Rāmānandīs. The Malūk Dāsīs worship Rāma as an incarnation of the Supreme and also use images. The main difference between this sect and that of the Rāmānandīs seems to be that the teachers of the Malūk Dāsīs are not ascetics, but, like their founder, laymen. Malūk Dās was a trader by occupation, and is said to have been born at Kaṛā, in the district of Allahābād, and to have died at Jagannāth. Monasteries of his followers at Kaṛā and other places are still in existence. The works ascribed to Malūk Dās include the following:—*Das Ratna* ("The Ten Jewels"); *Bhaktavatsal*, which deals with Krishṇa's regard for his devotees; *Ratna-khāna*, which is a dissertation on the soul and God. He is also the reputed author of a large number of detached verses and apophthegms which are still quoted amongst the people. A famous one is translated as follows, and has been compared with the teaching of St. Matt. vi. 26:

> **"The python doth no service, nor hath the fowl of the air a duty to perform (to earn its living);**
> **Quoth Malūk Dās, For all doth Rāma provide their daily bread."**

The idea of the couplet is based on the belief current in India that the python *(ajagara)* is unable to hunt for its food, but has to wait with its mouth open for its prey to walk into it.

Other Works connected with the Worship of Rama.— A disciple of Tulsī Dās, who was also his constant companion, was *Benī Mādhav Dās* (fl. 1600). He is said to have written a biography of his master called *Gosāīn Charitr*, and was also the author of other works, including a *Nakhśikh*. Besides the *Rāmāyaṇ* (or *Rām-charit-mānas*) and other works of Tulsī Dās dealing with the story of Rāma, there appeared during this period several other works connected with the same subject. *Chintāmaṇi Tripāṭhī* (fl. 1650), who is mentioned in the previous chapter as a writer on the art of poetry, also wrote a *Rāmāyaṇ* in *kavitta* and other metres.

Mān Dās (born 1623), of Braj, wrote a Hindī poem entitled *Rāmcharitr*, which is founded on two Sanskrit works, the *Rāmāyaṇa* of *Vālmīki* and the *Hanumān Nāṭaka*.

Īshwarī Prasād Tripāṭhī (fl. 1673) wrote the *Rām Bilās Rāmāyaṇ*, which is a translation of Vālmīki's poem.

Bāl Alī (fl. circ. 1692) was the author of two works both in praise of Rāma and Sītā and entitled *Nehprakāś* and *Sītā Rām Dhyānmañjari*. *Jānk Rasikī Śaran* (fl. 1703) wrote the *Avadh Sāgar*, which is a poem in honour of Rāma. *Bhagwant Rāy* (fl. 1750) was the ruler of Asothar, in the district of Fatehpur, and for several years resisted the attacks of the Mughal Emperor, ṭill he was killed by treachery in 1760. He was the author of a *Rāmāyaṇ*. Another work dealing with the story of Rāma was the *Rām Bilās* of *Śambhu Nāth* (fl. 1750). *Tulsī Sāhib* (1763-1843) was the eldest son of the Rājā of Poona, but was unwilling to succeed to the throne. He therefore left his kingdom and renounced the world, and becoming a wandering ascetic finally settled in Hāthras. Besides many hymns, he wrote a work called the *Ghaṭ-Rāmāyaṇ*. He claimed that in a previous birth he was none other than the great Tulsī Dās himself, and had in that birth composed the *Ghaṭ-Rāmāyaṇ*, but as it aroused a great deal of opposition it was not published to the world but the *Rām-charit-mānas* was substituted in its place. His work differs in style and language, as well as in subject matter, from that of his more-renowned namesake, and is decidedly inferior in character.

Madhu Sūdan Dās (fl. circ. 1782), who was a poet of considerable merit, was the author of the *Rāmāśvamedh*, in which he describes the horse-sacrifice made by Rāma. Like Tulsī Dās he was a devotee of Rāma, and his poetry resembles that of the great master.

Maniyār Singh, also called *Yār* (fl. circ. 1785), was another devotee of Rāma who was a skilful poet. He was a Kshatriya, of Benares. His works include the *Saundarya Laharī*, the *Sundarkāṇḍ*, and the *Hanumān Chhabbīsi*, all of which deal with some of the legends regarding Rāma and Hanumān.

Gaṇesh (fl. 1800), who was patronised by the Rājā of Benares, besides other poetical works, composed in Hindī verse a translation of part of Vālmīki's *Rāmāyaṇa*.

VII.

THE SUCCESSORS OF KABĪR

The Kabirpanthis.—The great influence which the teaching of Kabīr exercised is shown by the large number of sects which owe their origin to the ideas which he promulgated. These sects have their literature in the vernacular. The Kabīrpanthīs, who trace their direct origin to Kabīr, have two divisions. One has its centre at the Kabīr-chaurā in Benares, and is also associated with Maghar where Kabīr died. The other has its centre in Chhattīsgarh in the Central Provinces. Each of these divisions is ruled by a *mahant*, and each has its literature. The descent of the Benares *mahants* is traced back to Surat Gopāl, and that of the Chhattīsgarh *mahants* to Dharm Dās. These are sometimes said to have been personal disciples of Kabīr, but probably lived a little later. Although the Kabīrpanthīs have as a whole kept free from the worship of images, Hindu influence has in various ways found its way back into the sect. Kabīr rejected the doctrine of divine incarnation, but he himself is often now regarded as an incarnation of the Supreme. Hindu practices which he condemned, such as the use of the rosary, have been introduced. Except the works ascribed to Kabīr himself the large amount of literature belonging to this sect has been scarcely examined by those outside the sect. The *Bījak*, already mentioned in connection with Kabīr, was probably compiled about fifty years after his death. Two other works belonging to this sect may also be mentioned. These are the *Sukh Nidhān*, which probably belongs to about the middle of the eighteenth century, and the *Amar Mūl*, which is probably as late as 1800. A Kabīrpanthī who flourished about 1800 and wrote some pithy verses in *kuṇḍaliya* metre was *Palṭu Sāhib*.

The Sikhs.—It has already been mentioned in a previous chapter that the religion of the Sikhs, founded by Nānak, was greatly influenced by the teaching of Kabīr. Nānak was followed by nine *gurus* most of whom were poets. The sacred book of the Sikhs, called the *Granth Sāhib* (or sometimes the *Ādi Granth*, *i.e.* "Original Granth," to distinguish it from the later *Granth of the Tenth Guru*), was compiled in 1604 by Guru Arjun (1563-1606), who was the sixth Guru of the Sikhs. It contains the compositions of Guru *Nānak*, Guru *Aṅgad*, Guru *Amar Dās*, Guru *Rām Dās*, Guru *Arjun*, Guru *Teg Bahādur* (the ninth Guru) and a couplet of Guru *Govind Singh* (the tenth Guru). The compositions of these last two Gurus were added after the first compilation. Besides the writings of these Gurus, the *Granth* also contains panegyrics of the Gurus by the bards who attended on them or admired their characters, and hymns of several *bhagats*, such as Nāmdev, Kabīr and others, whose teachings corroborated that of the Gurus. The hymns are not arranged in the *Granth* according to their authors but according to the thirty-one *Rāgs*, or musical measures, to which they were composed. All the Gurus, except the last, adopted the name of Nānak as their *nom de plume*. At the beginning of the volume is placed the *Japjī*, which was composed by Nānak, and then follow the *So-Daru*, the *So-purkhu*, and the *Sohilā*, which are extracts from later parts of the books. All these pieces were intended for devotional purposes, and therefore placed at the beginning of the book. After the *Rāgs* at the end of the volume is the *Bhog*, or conclusion, which contains *ślokas* and panegyrics. The whole forms a lengthy volume, the ideas which it contains being repeated in endless variation. For the Sikhs it is a hymn-book and prayer-book as well as a manual of theology. The language varies in different parts, but for the most part the hymns are written in old dialects of Hindī with some admixture of Panjabī. A hymn of Guru Nānak was given in a previous chapter. The following is one of the hymns of Guru Arjun:—

"On the way where the miles cannot be counted,
The name of God shall there be thy provision;
On the way where there is pitch darkness,
The name of God shall accompany and light thee;
On the way where nobody knoweth thee,
The name of God shall be there to recognise thee;
Where there is very terrible heat and great sunshine,
There the name of God shall be a shadow over thee;
There, *saith* Nānak, *the name of* God shall rain nectar on thee."

The tenth Guru, whose name was *Govind Singh*, held office from 1675 to 1708. It was he who developed the Sikhs into a great military order called the Khālsā and organized them to resist the Muhammadans. Under him many Hindu ideas were introduced into the religion of the Sikhs. Govind Singh composed many verses mostly in Hindī (Braj Bhāshā), but some also in Persian and Panjābī. These works, together with the translations and other verses of some in the Guru's employ, were collected in the year 1734, after Govind Singh's death, by Bhai Mani Singh into one volume, which is called the *Granth of the Tenth Guru* to distinguish it from the *Ādi Granth*. It is used for the promotion of valour and other purposes, but it is not regarded by the Sikhs as having the same authority as the *Ādi Granth*. Besides the *Jāpjī*, or hymns, in praise of God, and many other religious verses, it contains the *Vichitr Nāṭak*, which is an account of the life and mission of Govind Singh, and other poems calculated to stir up the martial valour of the Sikhs.

The Dadupanthis.—The founder of the sect of Dādūpanthīs was Dādū (1544-1603), who was born at Ahmedābād, but spent most of his life in Rajputana. According to common report he was a cotton-carder by caste, but the tradition of his followers that he

[1] Translation by Macauliffe, "The Sikh Religion," Vol. III. 202.

was a Brahman is probably correct. His spirit of forgiveness and kindness (*dayā*) was so great that he was called Dādū Dayāl. His teaching is very similar to that of Kabīr, but is not so much affected by Muhammadan ideas. Much of the Hinduism against which Dādū protested has found its way back into the sect. Dādū rejected, for instance, the teaching of the Vedānta, caste, and idolatry, but some of his modern followers are Vedāntists, and only twice-born Hindus are allowed to read the *Bānī*, and the sect has no dealings at all with outcastes. Moreover, Dādū's *Bānī* is worshipped with idolatrous rites. Dādū's teaching was spread by fifty-two disciples. His doctrines are contained in the *Bānī*, a book of about five thousand verses. It is divided into thirty-seven chapters dealing with such subjects as the Divine Teacher, Remembrance, Separation, The Meeting, The Mind, Truth, The Good, Faith, Prayer, etc. The verses of Dādū are very attractive and have a musical rhythm, and hymns which are included amongst them are set to music and used both for public and private worship. The following is a translation of a few of Dādū's verses :—

"Receive that which is perfect into your hearts to the exclusion of all besides; abandon all things for the love of God, for this Dādū declares is the true devotion.

"Cast off pride, and become acquainted with that which is devoid of sin. Attach yourselves to Rāma, who is sinless, and suffer the thread of your meditations to be upon him.

"All have it in their power to take away their own lives, but they cannot release their souls from punishment; for God alone is able to pardon the soul, though few deserve His mercy.

"Listen to the admonitions of God, and you will care not for hunger nor for thirst; neither for heat, nor cold; ye will be absolved from the imperfections of the flesh.

"Draw your mind forth, from within, and dedicate it to God; because if ye subdue the imperfections of your flesh, ye will think only of God.

"If ye call upon God, ye will be able to subdue your imperfections, and the evil inclinations of your mind will depart from you; but they will return to you again when ye cease to call upon him.

"Dādū loved Rāma incessantly; he partook of his spiritual essence and constantly examined the mirror, which was within him.

"He subdued the imperfections of the flesh, and overcame all evil inclinations; he crushed every improper desire, wherefore the light of Rāma will shine upon him."[1]

The sect which Dādū founded has a very large literature in Hindī. Dādū's two sons were poets, and all his fifty-two disciples are reported to have composed verses, as well as many later followers. The most important poet amongst his disciples was *Sundar Dās* the younger (fl. 1620-1650), who is also called *Būsar*. By the Dādūpanthīs he is regarded as one of the best Hindī poets, worthy to rank amongst the highest names in Hindī literature. He was a voluminous writer. Amongst his most admired works are his *Savaiyas* (sometimes called the *Sundar Bilās*) and the *Gyān Samudra*. *Niśchal Dās*, a later Dādūpanthī poet, introduced Vedāntic ideas into the teaching of the sect.

The Lal Dasis.—*Lāl Dās*, who died in 1648, was the founder of a sect known as the Lāl Dāsīs. He belonged to Alwar, and came from a predatory tribe called the Meos. Like other teachers whose doctrines can be traced to Kabīr's influence he emphasized the value of the repetition of the name of Rāma. His teaching and hymns are contained in a work called the *Bānī*. The members of the sect often sing the hymns to music.

The Sadhs.—The sect of the Sādhs was founded in 1658 by *Bīr Bhān*, and is found chiefly in the upper part of the Doab. Bīr Bhān claimed to have received his doctrines from a superhuman instructor in the form of verses (*śabdas*) and couplets (*sākhīs*). These were collected into a volume called the *Ādi Upadeśa* ("Original Instruction"). These verses, together with those of other teachers like Kabīr, Nānak and Dādū, are recited at the meetings of the sect.

Dharni Das.—*Dharnī Dās* was born in 1656 and lived at the village of Māñjhī in the district of Chhaprā. He was a Kāyasth by caste, and became a devotee. He founded a sect which still survives. He is the

[1] Translation by G. R. Siddons, in the Journal of the Asiatic Society of Bengal, Vol. VI. (1837).

reputed author of two Hindī works, the *Satya Prakāś* and the *Prem Prakāś*.

Some Sufi Poets.—A Muhammadan who wrote Hindī verses was *Yārī Sāhib* (1668-1723). He seems to have been a Sūfī, and lived and taught at Delhi. Some of his disciples also wrote Hindī verse, such as *Keśav Dās* and *Bullā Sāhib*, both of whom flourished about 1730. A disciple of Bullā Sāhib was *Gulāl Sāhib*, and the latter had a disciple called *Bhīkhā Sāhib*. Both of these flourished in the latter half of the eighteenth century, and both are the reputed authors of Hindī verse. Two other Hindī writers who may have been connected with the same, or a similar movement, are *Dariyā Sāhib* of Bihār, and *Dariyā Sāhib* of Māṛwār. Both of these were Muhammadans and flourished in the first half of the eighteenth century. Another Muhammadan writer of Hindī verse who also lived in the first half of the eighteenth century was *Bulle Shāh*, and was probably a Sūfī.

The Charan Dasis.—Charan Dās (1703-1782) belonged to the *Ḍhūsar* caste of *Baniyas*. About the year 1730 he founded a sect at Delhi, which still exists. He had many disciples who spread his teaching, and he admitted as disciples not only men but women also. His teaching is very similar to that of Kabīr, and emphasizes such doctrines as the value of the repetition of the name of God, the importance of the word (*śabda*), the need of devotion (*bhakti*), and the necessity of having a *guru*. Idolatry was denounced by Charan Dās, but has crept back into the sect. The *guru* holds a very important place in the sect and is regarded as divine. Like similar sects it has a large literature in Hindī, and great stress is laid on this amongst its members, the use of Sanskrit being discouraged. The sect possesses translations in Hindī of the *Bhāgavata Purāṇa* and the *Bhagavad Gītā*, which are said to have been made, at least in part, by Charan Dās himself. Charan Dās also composed many other Hindī works which are much esteemed by his followers. Two of his women disciples were poetesses. These were *Sahajo Bāī* and *Dayā Bāī.* They are said to have been sisters and to have belonged to the same caste as Charan Dās. Their verses are of considerable merit and full of devotion. The *Dayā Bodh* of Dayā Bāī was composed in 1751.

The Siv Narayanis.—*Śiv Nārāyaṇ* was a Rajput who lived near Ghazipur. In 1734 he founded a sect which worships God as Brahman without attributes, and rejects idolatry. Śiv Nārāyaṇ is himself regarded as an incarnation by his followers. Outward conformity to the observances of Hindus and Muhammadans is permitted and people of all castes are admitted as members. It is said that the Emperor Muhammad Shāh (1719-1748) became a member of the sect. The founder was a voluminous writer and is credited with having composed sixteen books of Hindī verse.

The Garib Dasis.—The *guru* of *Garīb Dās* (1717-1782) is said to have been Kabīr, which, although an anachronism, seems to show that the sect he founded sprang from the Kabīrpanthīs. This sect, which is still in existence, consists only of *sādhūs*, who must belong to the twice-born castes. The book which he composed, called the *Guru Granth Sāhib*, contains 24,000 *sākhīs* and *chaupāīs.* Of these, however, 7,000 are said to be *sākhīs* of Kabīr. Garīb Dās lived at the village of Chhuṛanī in the Rohtak district of the Panjāb.

The Ram Sanehis.—The sect of Rām Sanehīs was founded by *Rām Charan* (born 1718), who lived in Rajputana. He was at first an idolater, but gave up the worship of idols and founded the sect of *Rām Sanehīs*, or "*Lovers of Rām*," The sect is now represented merely by an order of *sādhūs.* His sayings and hymns have been collected into a *Bānī.* The third leader of the sect, named *Dulhā Rām*, who became a Rām Sanehī in 1776, composed about 10,000 *śabdas* and 4,000 *sākhīs.* He died in 1824.

The Satnamis and Jagjivan Das.—The sect of the Satnāmīs seems to have been founded before the middle of the seventeenth century, but the circumstances of its origin are unknown. It was reorganised about 1750 by *Jagjīvan Dās*, who lived at Kotwa, between Lucknow and Ayodhyā. As the name of the sect implies, they adore the True Name alone, the one God, who is without attributes, but the Hindu pantheon is recognised and the Hindu incarnations regarded as the manifestations of God. Jagjīvan Dās is said to have been a Kshatriya by caste, but the sect has spread mostly amongst the outcastes. The Hindī verses of Jagjīvan Dās are in several works, which include the *Pratham Granth*, the *Mahāpralay*, and the *Gyān Prakāś*. A disciple of Jagjīvan named *Dulan Dās*, who lived in the district of Rai Bareilly, was also a Hindī poet. Other successors of Jagjīvan who wrote Hindī verse were *Jalālī Dās* and *Devī Dās*. A development of the Satnāmī sect occurred in Chhattīsgarh, in the Central Provinces, under a certain Ghāzi Dās, between 1820 and 1830. He introduced the ideas of the sect amongst the *chamārs* of that district though he did not acknowledge his indebtedness to Jagjīvan.

The Pran Nathis.—*Prāṇ Nāth* lived at Pannā in Bundelkhaṇḍ at the beginning of the eighteenth century, under the patronage of Rājā Chhatrasāl. He was the founder of a small sect in which not only Hindu and Muhammadan but also Christian influences were at work. By caste Prāṇ Nāth was a Kshatriya, but he was versed in Muhammadan as well as in Hindu learning, and he endeavoured to reconcile the two religions. The members of his sect are sometimes called Dhāmīs, from Dhām, a name they give to the Supreme spirit. They eat in common, but continue to observe the Hindu or Muhammadan practices of their own families. The works of Prāṇ Nāth are fourteen in number, all in verse, but none of them of very great length. Though the grammatical structure is purely Hindī, the vocabulary is very largely Arabic or Persian, and the language is very uncouth.

General Characteristics.—All the writers who are mentioned in this chapter wrote in that poetic style which is classified by Indian authorities as quietistic (*śānta ras*). Much of their verse is smooth and rhythmical, and the artistic influences which had come into Hindī literature were no doubt felt by them to a certain extent. But their interest was religious rather than literary, and few of them rank high amongst Hindī poets. If their verses are less rugged than those of Kabīr, they are also often lacking in the vigour and charm which characterise his work. The subjects dealt with in these voluminous works are not very extensive. The need of a *guru* and the respect due to him, the value of the repetition of the name of God, the supreme importance of devotion (*bhakti*), the delusions of *māyā*, the value of truth, the duty of living a righteous and sober life, these and a few kindred topics are repeated over and over again, in different ways, at interminable length, in a manner which to the ordinary reader is apt to be tedious. Nevertheless there are many striking passages to be found which are full of beauty and inculcate valuable lessons. During the greater part of this period the North of India was passing through a time of great political change. The reign of Aurangzeb (1658-1707) was a long struggle against disintegrating forces, and after him the political disorder grew worse. Internecine strife and rebellion were frequent. The invasions of Nādir Shāh (1739) and afterwards of Ahmad Shāh Durrānī (1756) were a time of terrible disaster. The Marāṭhas also were constantly attacking the Mughal Empire, which by the end of this period ceased to exist except in name. It was a time of frequent calamity, of persecution and tyranny; but during this period many thoughtful men sought peace of heart in piety and quietism, and it was in such circumstances that much of the religious verse referred to in this chapter was produced. In these poems the writers not only expressed their own aspiration and feeling after God, but gave forth many beautiful thoughts which were a solace to others in times of distress, and an incentive to them to live nobly and to seek after the highest ends. The sects whose literature is described in this chapter all owe something to Kabīr, in some cases the influence being direct and in others indirect. They all stand, in theory at least, for a non-idolatrous theism, and a great many of their theological conceptions are the same as, or similar to, those which Kabīr taught.

VIII.

THE KṚISHṆA CULT

(1550-1800)

The Ashta Chhap.—Vallabhāchārya and his son Viṭṭhalnāth, who have been mentioned in a previous chapter as the early leaders of the Vallabhāchārī sect at Gobardhan, near Muttra, each had four disciples, all of whom were Hindī poets. They are known as the *Ashṭa Chhāp*, or the Eight Seals, or Diestamps, because the poems they produced are regarded as standards for that dialect of Western Hindī in which they wrote. This dialect was the Braj Bhāshā, named after the district in which they lived, namely Muttra and Brindāban and the surrounding country. Since their time almost all Hindī poetry connected with the Kṛishṇa Cult has been composed in Braj Bhāshā, and it has also come to be looked upon as the poetic dialect of Hindī *par excellence*, though Tulsī Dās and most of the worshippers of Rāma wrote in Eastern Hindī. The disciples of Vallabhāchārya who are included in the *Ashṭa Chhāp* were *Sūr Dās*, *Kṛishṇa Dās Pay Ahārī*, *Parmānand Dās* and *Kumbhan Dās.* Those of Viṭṭhalnāth were *Chaturbhuj Dās*, *Chhīt Svamī*, *Nand Dās* and *Govind Dās.* All these flourished about the middle or second half of the sixteenth century.

Kṛishṇa Dās Pay Ahārī seems to have been a rival of Sūr Dās, though not equal to him in poetical merit. He was, however, the writer of graceful and melodious stanzas. His best known work is called the *Premsattvanirūp.* Kṛishṇa Dās had several pupils who became poets. According to some one of them was

Agra Dās (fl. 1575), who was in turn the preceptor of Nābhā Dās, author of the *Bhaktamālā*.

Nand Dās holds, next to Sur Dās, the highest place as a poet amongst those who are included in the *Ashṭa Chhāp*. He was a Brahman, and some have believed him to be a brother of the great Tulsī Dās. There is a proverb about him which says, *Aur sab gaṛiyā, Nand Dās jaṛiyā*, "All others are simply founders (or melters), but Nand Dās is the artificer (who joins the pieces of metal into a composite whole)." He was the author of several larger works as well as of detached verses. One of his compositions is a poem in imitation of the Sanskrit *Gītā Govinda*, called *Panchādhyāyī*.

Sur Das.—The greatest of all the *Ashṭa Chhāp*, however, was *Sūr Dās*. The particulars of his life are very scanty and uncertain. It is said that he was a Brahman and the son of Bābā Rām Dās, who was a singer at the court of the Emperor Akbar. At the age of eight he went with his parents to Muttra, and became the pupil of a devotee. Afterwards he removed to Gaū Ghāṭ, between Agra and Muttra, where he became a disciple of Vallabhāchāryā. In the commentary which he himself wrote to some of his emblematic verses he says that he was a descendant of the famous bard Chand Bardāī, that his father's name was Rām Chandra, and that his grandfather, Hari Chandra, lived at Agra. Some, however, consider him to be a Brahman and regard the verse where this information is given as spurious. His father lived at Gopchal and had seven sons, six of whom were killed in battle with the Muhammadans. He alone, blind (either literally or figuratively) and worthless, as he says, remained alive. He had a vision of Kṛishṇa, and thereafter "all was darkness" to him, which may mean he became blind. He went to live at Braj, and became one of the *Ashṭa Chhāp*. Tradition places his birth in 1483 and his death in 1563, but these dates are uncertain. All the traditions agree as to his blindness, either from birth, or from a later period of his life, and he is often referred to as "the blind bard of Agra."

Sūr Dās excelled in many styles of composition. A large number of episodes and passages from the *Bhāgavata Purāṇa* were reproduced by him in exquisite verse, and he was the writer of a great number of lyrics in connection with the worship of Kṛishṇa and Rādhā, which were collected together in the *Sūr Sāgar* and the *Sūrāvalī*. The *Sāhityalaharī* contains emblematic verses (*Dṛishṭakūṭ*), for which Sūr Dās himself wrote an explanatory commentary. He also wrote in Hindī the story of *Nala and Damayantī*. Altogether he is credited with having composed as many as 75,000 verses. Sūr Dās holds a very high place in literature. Some Indian authorities would give him the foremost place amongst Hindī poets, though most persons would reserve that honour for Tulsī Dās. An often quoted couplet referring to Hindi poetry says, "Sūr is the sun, Tulsī the moon, Keśav Dās is a cluster of stars, but the poets of to-day are like so many glow-worms giving light here and there." Sūr Dās is undoubtedly a poet of great power. He is considered to excel in his use of all the ornaments of style recognized by the authorities on Hindī poetry and in his use of images and similes. An anonymous poet of Akbar's court said with regard to him, "Gaṅg excels in sonnets and Bīrbal in the *kavitta* metre; Keśav's meaning is ever profound, but Sūr possesses the excellency of all three."

A few specimens of his work are given here :—

All days are not alike;
One day King Hariśchandra had in his power wealth like Mount Meru;
The next day he went to live in the house of a Chāndāl, and removed clothes from the burying-ground.
One day a man is a bridegroom, attended by a bridal company, and in every direction flags are placed;
The next day he has to live in the forest, and there stretches forth hands and legs.
One day Sītā is crying in a very terrible forest;
The next day having become re-united with Rāmchandra, both go about in a balloon of flowers.
One day Rājā Yudhishṭhir was reigning with Śrī Bhagwān (Kṛishṇa) as his follower;
The next day (his wife) Draupadī is made naked, and Duśāsan takes away her clothes.

The doings of the former birth appear; O foolish mind, give up anxiety;
Sūr Dās says, "How far can I describe the qualities? True are letters written by the Creator (on the forehead)."

* * * * *

Without Gopāl these bowers become like enemies.
In those days (when he was here) these creepers seemed very cool,
Now they have become a heap of fiery flames.
In vain the River Jamunā is flowing, and the birds twitter;
In vain the lotuses are blooming, and the black bee hums;
Sūr Dās says, "Looking for the lord, my eyes have become red like the *ghunghchī* seed."

* * * * *

Night and day my eyes shed tears;
It is always the rainy season with me, since Śyām went away.
The collyrium does not stay on my eyes, my hands and my cheeks have become dark,
The cloth of my bodice never gets dry, because the heart in the midst of it is running like a stream of water.
My eyes have become rivers, my limbs tired, and the fixed stars are moving away.
Sūr Dās says, "Braj is now being submerged (in tears), why do you not deliver it?"

The Chaurasi Varta.—An important work which belongs to this period is the *Chaurāsī Vārtā* (or "Eighty-four Tales"), reputed to have been written by *Gokulnāth* (fl. 1568), the son of Viṭṭhalnāth. It is earlier in date than the *Bhaktamālā*, and whereas the *Bhaktamālā* contains accounts of devotees of various Vaishṇava sects, the *Chaurāsī Vārtā* is devoted exclusively to stories, mostly legendary, of the followers of Vallabhāchārya. It lays a great deal of stress on the erotic side of the Kṛishṇa legends. From the point of view of the literature it is very important as being written in prose, of which it is one of the earliest specimens. It is written in a very clear and easy style, and although written three hundred and fifty years ago the language used differs very little from the modern Braj dialect.

Other early Vallabhacharis.—Two or three other early members of the Vallabhāchārī sect who were Hindi poets must also be mentioned. *Bhagwān Hit* (fl. circ. 1574) is said to have been a disciple of

Viṭṭhalnāth. He was the author of some Kṛishṇaite lyrics of considerable merit. *Raskhān* (fl. 1614) was a Muhammadan at first and his name was then Sayyad Ibrāhīm. He became a worshipper of Kṛishṇa and wrote verses in his honour which are said to be full of devotion and sweetness. A disciple of Raskhān was *Qādir Baksh*, who also wrote Hindī poetry.

The Radha-Vallabhis.—A new sect was founded in Brindāban about 1585 known as the *Rādhā-Vallabhīs.* In this sect Rādhā is placed above Kṛishṇa as an object of devotion. Its founder was *Hari Vaṁśa* (also called *Hit Haribans*, or *Hit Jī*). His father was a Gauṛ Brahman named Vyāsa, who was in the service of the Muhammadan Emperor. Hari Vaṁśa wrote in Sanskrit the *Rādhā-sudhā-nidhi*, which consists of 170 couplets. His principal work in Hindī is the *Chaurāsī Pad* (or *Premlatā*). The erotic side of the Kṛishṇa cult is very prominent in these works and they are full of sensuous imagery, but Hari Vaṁśa possesses great skill as a poet and holds a high place in Hindī literature. A few stanzas are here given :—

"Whatever my Beloved doeth is pleasing to me; and whatever is pleasing to me, that my Beloved doeth. The place where I would be is in my Beloved's eyes; and my Beloved would fain be the apple of my eyes. My Love is dearer to me than body, soul, or life; and my Love would lose a thousand lives for me. Rejoice, Śrī Hit Hari Vans! the loving pair, one dark, one fair, are like two cygnets; tell us who can separate wave from water?

"O my Beloved, has the fair spoken? this is surely a beautiful night; the lightning is folded in the lusty cloud's embrace. O friend, where is the woman who could quarrel with so exquisite a prince of gallants? Rejoice, Śrī Hari Vans! dear Rādhikā hearkened with her ears and with voluptuous emotion joined in love's delight.

* * * * *

"Come Rādhā, you knowing one, your paragon of lovers has started a dance on the bank of the Jamunā's stream. Bevies of damsels are dancing in all the abandonment of delight; the joyous pipe gives forth a stirring sound. Near the Bansi-bat, a sweetly pretty spot, where the spicy air breathes with delicious softness, where the half-opened jasmine fills the world with overpowering fragrance, beneath the clear radiance of the autumnal full moon, the milkmaids with raptured eyes are gazing on your glorious lord, all beautiful from head to foot, quick to remove love's every pain. Put your arms about his neck, fair dame, pride of the world, and, lapped in the bosom of the Ocean of delight, disport yourself with Śyām in his blooming bower."[1]

Many members of this sect have been Hindī poets, amongst whom we may mention *Nāgarī Dās*, who flourished at the end of the sixteenth century, *Dhruv Dās* (fl. circ. 1630), who was a very voluminous writer, and *Śrī Hiṭ Brindāban Dās Jī Chāchā* (fl. 1743). All these were poets of some merit, especially the last, who wrote many verses of great beauty in praise of Kṛishṇa.

The Hari Dasis.—Another sect at Brindāban is that of the Hari Dāsīs. It was founded by Svāmī *Hari Dās*, who lived at the end of the sixteenth century and the beginning of the seventeenth century. His teaching seems to be closely akin to that of Chaitanya. Besides works in Sanskrit he left poems in Hindī. The best known are the *Sādhāran Siddhānt* and the *Ras Ke Pad*. Hari Dās possessed considerable merit as a poet. Here are a few stanzas of the *Sādhāran Siddhānt* :—

"Set your affection on the lotus-eyed, in comparison with whose love all love is worthless; or on the conversation of the saints: that so the sin of your soul may be effaced. The love of Hari is like the durable dye of the madder; but the love of the world is like a stain of saffron that lasts only for two days. Says Hari Dās, Set your affection on Bihārī, and he knowing your heart will remain with you for ever.

"A straw is at the mercy of the wind, that blows it about as it will and carries it whither it pleases. So is the realm of Brahma, or of Śiva, or this present world. Says Śrī Hari Dās: This is my conclusion, I have seen none such as Bihārī.

"Man is like a fish in the ocean of the world, and other living creatures of various species are as the crocodiles and alligators, while the soul like the wind spreads the entangling net of desire. Again, avarice is as a cage, and the avaricious as divers, and the four objects of life as four compartments of the cage. Says Hari Dās, Those creatures only can escape who ever embrace the feet of the son of bliss.

"Fool, why are you slothful in Hari's praises? Death goeth about with his arrows ready. He heedeth not whether it be in season or out of season, but has ever his bow on his shoulder. What avail heaps of pearls and other jewels and elephants tied up at your gate? Says Śrī Hari Dās, Though your queen in rich attire await you in her

[1] Translation from Mr. F. S. Growse's *Mathura*, pp. 196 ff.

chamber, all goes for nothing when the darkness of your last day draweth nigh." [1]

Hari Dās was succeeded as leader of the sect by *Viṭṭhal Vipul*, and the latter by *Bihārini Dās*. Both these were Hindī poets, Bihārini Dās being a very voluminous one. In his numerous verses he uses the most erotic language to express the intensity of his religious devotion. *Sītal* (fl. 1723), who was a leader of the sect, was also a skilful poet. *Sahachari Śaran* (fl. 1763) also belonged to the Hari Dāsīs. Amongst his works is the *Lalit Prakāś*, which contains sayings of Hari Dās, the founder of the sect.

Other Writers of Krishna Verse.—*Gadā Dhar Bhaṭṭ* (fl. 1565) was a Kṛishṇaite belonging to the sect of Chaitanya and wrote verses of considerable merit in Kṛishṇa's honour. *Bihārī Lāl Chaube*, whose work has been described in a previous chapter as a writer on the art of poetry, was also connected with the Kṛishṇa Cult. Most of the verses in his famous *Sat Saī* deal with some phase or other of the story of Kṛishṇa. Other writers on the art of poetry also wrote Kṛishṇaite verse.

Tāj, who flourished in the first half of the seventeenth century, was the wife of a Muhammadan, but was a worshipper of Kṛishṇa. She wrote some much admired verses in his honour.

Bhīshma (fl. circ. 1650) translated the famous tenth chapter of the *Bhāgavata Purāṇa* into Hindī verse, under the title *Bāl Mukund Līlā*.

Bakhshī Hansrāj (fl. 1732) was a Kāyasth of Pannā, who was a skilful poet. He wrote the *Saneh Sāgar*, which is an account of Rādhā and Kṛishṇa, as well as some other works.

Mān, a Brahman of Baiswāṛā, wrote in 1761 a translation of the *Kṛishṇa Khaṇḍa* entitled *Kṛishṇa Kallol*.

A famous work in connection with the Kṛishṇa Cult is the *Braj Bilās* (1770). It was the work of *Braj Bāsī Dās*, of Brindāban, and contains a description

[1] Translation from Mr. F.S. Growse's *Mathura*, p. 210.

of Kṛishṇa's life during his residence at Brindāban. Braj Bāsī Dās belonged to the sect of Vallabhāchārīs.

Sundari Kuñwari Bāī (fl. 1760 to 1798) was a princess of the Rāṭhor family, and daughter of Rāj Singh, Mahārāja of Rūpnagar and Kṛishṇagaṛh. She was married to Bal Bhadra Singh, Mahārāja of Rāghavgaṛh. Many of her family were poets, and this lady wrote a large number of poems full of religious devotion, many of which are in honour of Kṛishṇa.

Manchit Dvij (fl. circ. 1779), of Bundelkhaṇḍ, was the author of *Surbhīdānlīlā*, which is an account of the childhood of Kṛishṇa, and *Kṛishṇāyan*, which is a life of Kṛishṇa. His poems are considered to be of a very high standard of poetic excellence.

Bībī *Ratan Kuñwār*, of Benares, was born about 1842. She was the grandmother of Rājā Śiv Prasād, who helped to develop Hindī literature in the nineteenth century. In the *Prem Ratna* she has given an account of the devotees of Kṛishṇa, and in addition she was the authoress of many other verses.

General Remarks on Krishnaite Literature.—A great deal of the poetry connected with the Kṛishṇa Cult deals with the amours of Kṛishṇa with the Gopīs (milkmaids) of Braj, and especially with Rādhā. The great Hindu teachers of *bhakti* threw a mystical glamour over these stories. Kṛishṇa was to them the Supreme Deity, from whom all creation was but a sportive emanation, and who was full of love to his devotees. Rādhā and the other Gopīs stood for human souls, of whom Rādhā especially typified the devotee, ready to offer her whole self in devotion to God. In the literature connected with this form of the *bhakti* movement the writers often use the most erotic language and sensuous imagery to describe the soul's devotion, under the picture of Rādhā's self-abandonment to her beloved. Many of the verses could not be translated into English. Yet the writers of these lyrics of passionate devotion were often men of real religious earnestness, quite free from any impure motives in composing them. That literature of this kind has, however, a very dangerous tendency has too often been shown in the history of the Kṛishṇa movement.

Many of the writers mentioned in this chapter were poets of very high merit. The artistic influences which had come into Hindī literature are to be seen in a very marked degree in their work. Muttra, which was the centre of the movement, was in close proximity to the Mughal court, and Sūr Dās is said by tradition to have had some connection with the court. But, through whatever channel the influence came, there is no doubt that the poets of Braj felt very strongly the tendencies towards the perfection of the poetic art, and the excellency and fame of their poetry was so great that from their time onwards Braj Bhāshā came to be regarded as the chief poetic dialect of Hindī.

IX.

BARDIC AND OTHER LITERATURE

(1550-1800)

Bards of Mewar.—The succession of bards in the various kingdoms of Rajputana and other parts of Hindustan was continued right down to modern times, and Mewār was one of the states where great encouragement was given to them. A chronicle of the time of Rānā Jagat Singh, of Mewār, who reigned from 1628 to 1654, called the *Jagat Bilās*, was written by an unknown bard. The successor of Jagat Singh, Rānā Rāj Singh (1654-1681), who was the famous opponent of Aurangzeb, was a great patron of poets. The chronicle of his time, called *Rāj Prakāś*, was also written by an anonymous bard. At the suggestion of Rānā Rāj Singh his poet-laureate, *Mān* (fl. 1660), wrote the *Rāj Dev Bilās*, which describes the struggle between Aurangzeb and Rāj Singh. Another poet who lived at his court was *Sadāśiv* (fl. 1660), who wrote his patron's life under the title *Rāj Ratnākar*. The son of Rāj Singh was Rānā Jai Singh (1681-1700) and he also was a patron of poets. A work which he had written by poets at his court was the *Jai Dev Bilās*, which is a series of lives of the kings whom he had conquered. Another author of a bardic chronicle of Mewār, entitled *Rāj Pattanā*, was *Ran Chhor*, whose date is doubtful.

Bards of Marwar.—In Māṛwār also great patronage was given to poets. Mahārāja Sūr Singh is said in one day to have distributed six lakhs of rupees to six poets at his court. His son Gaj Singh was also a patron of poets, as well as his grandson Amar Singh.

Amar Singh quarrelled with his father and was exiled. He went to the court of the Emperor Shāh Jahān, but in revenge for a slight he attempted to murder the Emperor, and was cut down after killing a number of courtiers. Among the poets patronised by Amar Singh were *Banwārī Lāl*, who wrote a panegyric of his patron, and *Raghu Nāth Rāy*, both of whom flourished about 1634. Mahārāja Ajīt Singh, of Jodhpur in Māṛwār (1681-1724), had a work written entitled the *Rāj Rūpakākhyāt*, which contains a history of his family from the commencement of the solar race to 1724. *Karan* was the poet and bard of Jodhpur at the time of Mahārāja Abhay Singh (1724-1750), son of Ajīt Singh. In his poem, called the *Sūrya Prakāś*, he wrote a history of the period from 1638 to 1731 in 7,500 lines. Mahārāja *Vijai Singh*, who reigned at Jodhpur from 1753 to 1784, was himself a poet, and he also had a work written, entitled the *Vijai Bilās*, which gives an account in 100,000 couplets of the war between Vijai Singh and his cousin Rām Singh.

Bards at Other Courts.—Other courts also had their poets. The rebellion of Jagat Singh, of Mhow, against Shāh Jahān was celebrated by a bard named *Gambhīr Rāy* (fl. 1650). In honour of Rāv Ratan (fl. 1650), great-grandson of Rājā Uday Singh, an anonymous bard wrote a history called *Rāv Ratan Rāysā*. *Jai Singh Sawāī*, of Jaipur (reigned 1699-1743), was not only a patron of poets but wrote his own autobiography, entitled *Jai Singh Kalpadrum* Jai Singh Sawāī's brother-in-law, *Buddh Rāv*, Rājā of Būndī, was also a poet and a patron of poets. *Jodhrāj* (fl. 1728) was a Brahman, who wrote the *Hammīr Kāvya* at the orders of the Mahārāja of Nīmrāṇā, which deals with the same incidents formerly described by the bard Śārang Dhar, who lived in the fourteenth century. *Ghan Śyām Śukla* (fl. circ. 1680) attended the court of the Rājā of Rewah and wrote in his praise. He also attended the court of the Rājā of Benares. His poems are considered to be of great merit. *Harikesh* (fl. 1731) attended the court of Rājā Chhatrasāl, of

Pannā. He excelled in the heroic style. *Sūdan* (fl. 1750) was a Brahman, who was patronised by Sūraj Mal, a son of the Mahārāja of Bharatpur. He wrote the *Sujān Charitr*, which is an account of the battles in which Sūraj Mal took part. Sūdan is considered to be an excellent narrative poet, especially in his account of the preparations for a battle, but he was not equal to Lāl Kavi in his description of the battle itself. A bard who wrote in the Maithilī dialect of Bihārī was *Lāl Jhā* (fl. 1780), one of the most famous poets of Mithilā. He was the author of a poem called *Kanarpī Ghāṭ Laṛāī*, which is a description of the battle of Kanarpī Ghāṭ, in which his patron Mahārāja Narendra Singh, of Darbhangā, was victorious.

Lal Kavi.—At the court of Rājā Chhatrasāl (1646-1731), who ruled at Pannā in Bundelkhaṇḍ and was himself a poet, much encouragement was given to men of letters. The most famous of these was *Lāl*, generally known as *Lāl Kavi.* His full name was *Gorelāl Purohit.* Besides writing a treatise on lovers, he wrote in Braj Bhāshā verse a celebrated work entitled *Chhatra Prakāś.* It gives an account of the wars and order of succession of the ancient Rājās of Bundelkhaṇḍ, and the life of Chhatrasāl and that of his father are related with great detail. Lāl Kavi achieved great excellence as a narrative poet, especially in his description of a battle. The following is the account in the *Chhatra Prakāś* of Rājā Chhatrasāl's bravery at the battle of Deogarh :—

"Rājā Chhatrasāl, valiant in war, dreadful in battle, famed for heroic achievements, active, vigorous, and powerful as a tiger, penetrated into the midst of the Deogarh Rājā's army ; while thousands of balls and arrows discharged at him fell like rain around. Firm and undaunted, redoubling his efforts he furiously attacked the numerous troops by whom he was surrounded. Entirely disregarding balls and bullets, he inflicted and received wounds in the enemy's ranks. The foe was confounded. The gods were amazed at the fighting of Chhatrasāl ; and, while repelling the attack of thousands, and scattering death and destruction around, Kālī delighted to see his sword-dance. His progress no one could stop ; for, as soon as an antagonist had raised his sword, Chhatrasāl, by superior dexterity, inflicted a wound ; and he was equally skilful in the use of the spear. Separated from his troops, and surrounded by foes, he fought his way from one flank of their army to the other. Wherever he went, victory followed. Disregarding severe wounds, he renewed the attack, fighting with such impetuosity and fury, that the enemy, believing him to be Kāl Rudra, took to flight, and abandoned the field. Chhatrasāl obtained lasting fame and renown: for the enemy fled like deer from a tiger. The kettle-drums sounded strains of victory, and Bahādūr Khān ordered the camp to be pitched.''[1]

Other Literature of the Period.—Besides the literature we have already mentioned in this and the preceding chapters, there were many other writers on a variety of subjects during the period. There are works dealing with the philosophy of the Vedānta, works connected with the Jain religion, works on morals (*nīti*), comic verses, and a great many other topics, including text-books on such subjects as lexicography, agriculture, astronomy, and veterinary surgery. A few of the authors may be mentioned here :—

Nāth Kavi (b. 1584), who dwelt in Braj, wrote poems on the seasons and other subjects.

Mubārak Alī (b. 1583), of Bilgrām in the district of Hardoī, was the author of a large number of short verses which are still current.

Nāzir (fl. before 1600), of Agra, was a versatile poet of considerable fame whose verses are very popular and often quoted, though many of them are said to be indecent.

Banārsī Dās (b. 1586) was a follower of the Jain religion. He lived at Jaunpur and died sometime after 1641. His works are full of religious teaching and he is much admired as a poet. In his most famous work he gives an account of his own life.

Srī Dhar (b. 1623), of Rajputana, was the author of a work in honour of Durga and entitled *Bhawānī Chhand*.

Ghāsī Rām (fl. circ. 1623) was a poet of considerable merit, who wrote on love, morals and other subjects.

Puhakar (fl. 1634) was a Kāyasth who lived during the time of Jahāngīr. He was in prison for some offence and while there composed the *Ras Ratan*.

[1] Translation by W. R. Pogson, *A History of the Boondelas*.

When Jahāngīr heard of this he pardoned him. The poem is in the form of a story.

Dāmodar Dās (fl. circ. 1660) belonged to the sect of the Dādūpanthīs. He translated the *Mārkaṇḍeya Purāṇa* into Rājasthānī. This work is of interest as being in prose instead of verse.

Chhatra (fl. 1700), a Kāyasth of Anṭer village in Gwalior, was the author of the *Vijai Muktāvalī*. This is an abstract of the *Mahābhārata* in Hindī verse.

Sabal Singh (b. 1670) belonged to a ruling family. He also was the author of a condensed metrical translation of 24,000 verses of the *Mahābhārata*.

Baitāl (b. 1677) attended the court of Vikram Sāhi. He wrote moral and occasional verses and, though no complete work of his is extant, his verses are much admired.

Devi Dās (fl. 1685) belonged to Bundelkhaṇḍ. Under the patronage of Rājā Ratan Pāl Singh, of Karaulī, he wrote a much admired work on morals called *Prem Ratnākar*. He was also the author of numerous other works.

Motī Rām (b. 1683) was the author of the Braj Bhāshā version of a story called *Mādhonal*, which was afterwards translated into Urdu by *Lallū Jī Lāl*.

Bhū Dhar Dās (fl. 1724) was a Jain who wrote works connected with the Jain religion, including the *Jain Śatak* and the *Pārśva Purāṇ*. He is considered to possess considerable power as a poet.

Ghāgh (b. 1696), of Kanauj, wrote on the subject of agriculture. His aphorisms have a wide currency in North India.

Gaṅgā Pati (fl. 1719) was the author of a poem dealing with the different philosophical doctrines of the Hindus. It is called *Vigyān Bilās*, and is written in the form of a dialogue between a *guru* (teacher) and his *chela* (disciple). A mystic life based on the Vedānta philosophy is advocated.

Kripā Rām (fl. 1720) was an astronomer at the court of Rājā Jai Singh Sawāī, of Jaipur, and wrote a work in Hindī on astronomy.

Giri Dhar (b. 1713), of the Doab, wrote verses on morals (*nīti*) and occasional pieces which are much admired. He used the *kuṇḍaliya* metre of which some critics consider him to be the greatest master. His verses abound in colloquialisms and many of them have become proverbs.

Śrī Nāgarī Dās (fl. 1723) was Mahārāja of Kṛishṇagaṛh in Rajputana. His real name was Sāvat Singh, but he adopted the name of Nāgarī Dās as his *nom de plume*. He was a poet of considerable merit besides being a king of great valour.

Nūr Muhammad (fl.1743) was the author of the *Indrāvati*. It is a love story similar to the *Padumāvati* of *Malik Muhammad*. It is considered to be a well-written poem.

Manbodh Jhā (fl. 1750), also known as *Bholan Jhā*, of the district of Darbhāngā, was one of the most celebrated poets in the Maithilī dialect of Bihārī. He wrote a version of the *Harivaṁśa* of which only ten sections have been preserved. These, however, are very popular.

Nidhān (fl.1751) and *Dayā Nidhi* (b. 1754) each wrote a treatise on veterinary surgery under the title *Śālihotr*.

Rām Chandra was a Brahman who flourished at the end of the eighteenth century. He wrote a work in five books in honour of the feet of Pārvati, entitled *Charaṇ Chandrikā*. It is considered to be a work of great poetic merit.

X.

THE MODERN PERIOD

(From 1800)

A NEW influence came into Hindī literature at the beginning of the nineteenth century through contact with the culture of the West. The eighteenth century had been largely a time of literary dearth, but a renascence now began. The East India Company, which had commenced its career in India as a trading company, had now come into possession of a vast Empire and was beginning to feel its responsibilities towards those whom it was called upon to govern. This responsibility was being continually urged by many in the British Parliament. Amongst other responsibilities that were recognised was the duty of fostering and helping the culture and education of the peoples under the rule of the Company. The introduction of the printing-press helped to diffuse literary culture. The spread not only of vernacular but of English education could not but have a vast effect upon the life and thought of India. Just as in the case of the revival of learning in Europe the study of the Latin and Greek classics not only led to a stimulation of thought, but also helped to revive the literature of the European vernaculars, so also in India the study of English has been accompanied by a great renascence of the vernacular literature of India. The peace and security which the British rule brought to India, after the long period of internecine strife and disorder through which the country had been passing, also gave the genius of Hindī literature the opportunity of reasserting itself, and of recovering from the decay into which it had fallen in the eighteenth century. This period is marked by the creation of a new Hindī literary dialect and of Hindī prose.

Lallu Ji Lal.—At the commencement of the nineteenth century the head of the Fort William College at Calcutta was Dr. John Gilchrist. With the help of the other European officers of the College, such as Captain Abraham Lockett, Professor J. W. Taylor, and Dr. Hunter, he gave a great impetus to the cultivation of vernacular literature. Text-books suitable for the study of the European officials were collected, and a group of vernacular scholars gathered together and encouraged to produce new literature. Most of the work was in connection with the Urdu language, but *Lallū Jī Lāl*, who also wrote Urdu, and *Sadal Miśra*, did for Hindī what was being done by other scholars for Urdu. The works which they produced, if not the first prose works in those languages, were the first literary standards, and established prose as a recognised form of literature. Lallū Jī Lāl was a Brahman whose family had come originally from Gujarat, but had long been settled in North India. Under the direction of Dr. John Gilchrist he and Sadal Miśra were the creators of modern "High Hindī." Many dialects of Hindī were, as we have seen, spoken in North India, but the vehicle of polite speech amongst those who did not know Persian, was Urdu. Urdu, however, had a vocabulary borrowed largely from the Persian and Arabic languages, which were specially connected with Muhammadanism. A literary language for Hindī-speaking people which could commend itself more to Hindus was very desirable, and the result was produced by taking Urdu and expelling from it words of Persian or Arabic origin, and substituting for them words of Sanskrit or Hindī origin. The name *Khari Boli* ("pure speech") is sometimes used for the dialect of Delhi and Meerut, which was the language from which Urdu sprang, as well as for the modern Hindī literary dialect. It seems to be implied that Lallū Jī Lāl was only restoring the Delhi and Meerut dialect to its original purity and using it for literary purposes. This, however, was hardly the case, for though Urdu sprang originally from this dialect it had also assimilated many words of Panjābī and Rājasthānī as well as those of Arabic and Persian origin. The Hindī of Lallū Jī Lāl was really a new literary dialect. This "High Hindī," or "Standard Hindī" as it is also called, has had however a great success. It has been adopted as the literary speech of millions in North India. Poetical works still continue to be written in *Braj Bhāshā*, or *Avadhī*, or other old dialects, as High Hindī has not been much used for poetry. But whereas before this time prose works in Hindī were very rare, from now onwards an extensive prose literature began to be produced. The first work in this new dialect, and one which is regarded as a standard, was Lallū Jī Lāl's *Prem Sāgar*, which is a version of the tenth chapter of the *Bhāgavata Purāṇa*. It was founded on a previous Braj Bhāshā version of Chaturbhuj Miśra, and was begun in 1804 and completed in 1810. The *Rājnīti* (1809), which is also much admired for its language, was an adaptation of the *Hitopadeśa* and the *Pañchatantra*, and is in Braj Bhāshā. The *Singhāsan Battīsī* and the *Baitāl Pachīsī* are collections of stories in mixed Urdu and Hindī. Besides other works in Hindī and Urdu, Lallū Jī Lāl also wrote a commentary on the *Sat Saī* of Bihāri Lāl called *Lāl Chandrikā*, and gathered a collection of poems in Braj Bhāshā called *Sabhā Bilās*. *Sadal Miśra* (fl. 1803) was the author of the *Nāsketopākhyān*, which gives in Hindī prose the well-known story of Nachiketas.

Serampore.—In connection with the revival of Hindī literature mention must also be made of the work being done about this time by William Carey and his colleagues Ward and Marshman at Serampore. Amongst the many translations of the Christian Scriptures made by these missionaries were some in the dialects of North India. The Hindī version was Carey's own work. The first portions of his Hindī New Testament were published in 1809 and the Hindī translation of the whole Bible was completed in 1818. Besides translations of

.the Scriptures, Carey and his colleagues also printed editions of many vernacular works, amongst them being the *Rāmāyaṇ*. Most of these editions perished in a fire which destroyed the printing-press at Serampore in 1812. In 1818 Carey began to publish a newspaper in Bengali, which was the first newspaper printed in any oriental language, and was the forerunner of the many newspapers now issued from the vernacular press. All this work of Carey and his coworkers helped greatly in the development of vernacular literature.

Raja Siv Prasad.—The new literary dialect which Lallū Jī Lāl produced has not been without its critics. As it includes many Sanskrit words it is a speech not easy to be understood except by the learned. It tends to fall into the same extreme as Urdu. Rājā *Śiv Prasād* (1823-1895) is especially remembered as one who tried to popularise a literary speech midway between the Persian-ridden Urdu, and the Sanskrit-ridden High Hindī, which he believed to be nearer the colloquial speech of the people. The controversy is by no means settled yet. Rāj Śiv Prasād was the grandson of the poetess Bībī Ratan Kuṅwār. In his youth he was Vakīl to the Mahārāja of Bharatpur, but afterwards he entered the English service. He rose to the position of Nūr Munshi and became an Inspector in the Department of Public Instruction. He was eventually granted the hereditary title of Rājā. Besides translations and other works, all of which show the modern influence, he was the author of a great many text-books for schools.

The Printing-Press.—The outstanding feature of the development of Hindī literature in modern times has been the production of a very large number of works in prose. This has been very much facilitated by the use of the printing-press. It was at the College press at Fort William that printing was first used for Hindī works, but at first the expense hindered its rapid development, and the ungraceful characters of the type were not regarded with favour. The work of Carey and others at Serampore has already been mentioned. In 1837 a lithographic press was set up at Delhi, and from that date onwards the publication of books in Hindī has been increasing continually. The introduction of lithography was soon followed by the publication of Hindī newspapers and magazines, of which there are now a large number. All kinds of books have been turned out from the press—translations of English books, books and pamphlets dealing with religious and social questions, novels, educational text-books, and books on many other subjects; but it cannot be said with regard to most of them that a high literary standard has yet been reached, and experience alone will show how many of them are worthy to rank as standard works of Hindī literature. Hindī prose literature is still feeling its way, and its standards are not yet fixed. One book which has had probably a greater circulation than any other Hindī work in modern times (whether as a whole or in portions) is the Hindī translation of the Bible, and owing to its large circulation is bound to have an important influence on the life of the people. The printing-press has also been used to produce many of the older works of Hindī literature, which are now accessible to the general public in a way which was before impossible.

Harischandra.—That the new influence from the West revived rather than checked the cultivation of Hindī poetry is illustrated in the case of Bābū *Hariṣchandra* (1850-1885), of Benares, who is often called Bhāratendu ("The moon of India"). He was educated at Queen's College, Benares, and was a prolific and successful writer of poetry in many styles, having commenced to write at the age of sixteen. He wrote altogether about a hundred and seventy-five different works. Among these are eighteen plays, and Hariśchandra was the real founder of the modern drama in India. In his plays some of his best work is to be found, and they exhibit his great desire for the progress of India and the development of its intellectual freedom.

Hariśchandra wrote also on various subjects including history, patriotism, religious devotion, and love. He was also the author of many humorous verses. His historical works include the *Kāshmīr Kusum*, or history of Kashmīr, and the *Charitāvalī*, a series of lives of great men both Indian and European. Next to his plays his love poems are considered to be the best part of his work. Love and mirth are prominent characteristics of his poetry, which is full of power. He must be reckoned amongst the great writers of Hindī literature. He used chiefly the Braj Bhāshā dialect. Hariśchandra also did much to cultivate interest in Hindī poetry. To accomplish this he started a magazine called *Hariśchandrikā*, in which he published a number of old texts with much other matter. He also produced anthologies of Hindī poetry such as the *Sundarī Tilak*, which contains poems in the *savaiyā* metre from the works of sixty-nine poets, and the *Kavi Bachan Sudhā*, which is a collection of poems dealing with the rainy season.

As an example of the poetry of Hariśchandra the following translation is given:—

O warriors, having put on your arms, arise for the fight, and fly the flag of victory;
Draw your sword from the scabbard, and join the battle.
Having girded up your loins, put your arrow to your bow;
Put on your saffron-coloured garments and the bracelet of battle (as sign of a vow to conquer or die);
If the Aryans be united, and think of their own dignity,
They will give up quarrels amongst themselves, and support the honour of their race.
Then the strength of the mean Amīrkhān cannot be great.
When a lion is roused, can a dog stand in battle against him?
Even an ant trampled underfoot bites, although it is only insignificant.
These are visible enemies, woe to those who ignore them.
Woe to those who, being Aryans, have a love to those who are barbarians.
Woe to those who have any dealings with them.
Warriors, arise, and having put on all your weapons, plunge into the battle.
Write with a pen of steel the strength of the Aryans on the heart of both (conquerors and conquered).

The Hindī and Bihārī Drama.—The Hindī drama is of very recent origin. Some earlier writers produced what are called *nāṭaks*, or plays. Among these were Dev (fl. 1700), the author of *Dev Māyā Prapanch;* Newāj (fl. 1700), who wrote the Śakuntalā; Brāj Bāsī Dās (fl. 1770), who wrote the *Probodh Chandroday*, and some others. But their works were either without entrances and exits of the characters, or lacking in other essentials of dramatic poetry. The first real play in Hindī was the *Nahush Nāṭak*, written by *Gopāl Chand* (alias *Giri Dhar Dās*) in 1857. It deals with Indra's expulsion from his throne by Nahush and his subsequent reinstatement. Next came the *Śakuntalā* (1862) of Rājā *Lakshman Singh* (1826-1899), which is very famous and much admired. *Hariśchandra* then began to write dramas, his first being *Vidyā Sundar*. He wrote eighteen altogether. Other writers of Hindī drama were *Śrīnivās Dās*, *Totā Rām*, *Gopāl Rām*, *Kāśī Nāth Khattrī*, *Purohit Gopī Nāth*, *Lālā Sītā Rām*, besides many others. The first Hindī play was performed in 1868.

In Bihār the dramatic tradition is very much older. *Vidyāpati Ṭhākur*, who belongs to the middle of the fifteenth century, is reputed to be the author of two plays. *Lāl Jhā* (fl. 1780) wrote a play called *Gaurī Pariṇay*. In the early part of the nineteenth century *Bhānu Nāth Jhā* wrote the *Prabhāvati Haraṇ* and later *Harsh Nāth Jhā* wrote the *Ushā Haraṇ*. The Bihārī drama, however, differs from the Hindī in one very important feature, for the characters speak in Sanskrit and Prākrit, and only the songs are written in the Maithilī dialect.

Anthologies.—The revival of interest in Hindī literature and its appeal through the printing-press to a wider public is illustrated by the large number of anthologies of Hindī verse which have appeared in this period. Besides those of Lallū Jī Lāl and Hariśchandra, which have already been mentioned, the following may be noted :—

The *Rāg-Sagarodbhāv Rāg Kalpadrum* contains selections from the works of more than two hundred poets. It is a very voluminous work and was compiled by a Brahman named *Kṛishṇānand Vyās Dev*, and completed in 1843.

The *Ras Chandroday*, which is a collection of poems by two hundred and forty-two poets, was compiled in 1863 by *Ṭhākur Prasād Tripāṭhī*.

The *Dig-Vijai Bhūshaṇ* was compiled in the year 1869 by a Kāyasth, of Balirāmpur in the district of Gonda, named *Gokul Prasād*. It contains selections from the works of a hundred and ninety-two poets.

The *Śiv Singh Saroj* was compiled from former anthologies by *Śiv Singh Seṅgar*. The second edition of this very valuable work was published in 1883.

Gokul Nath.—A famous work belonging to this period was the translation of the Mahābhārata into Hindī verse. This was begun by *Gokul Nāth* (fl. 1820), of Benares, being undertaken at the instance of Rājā Udit Nārāyaṇ, of Benares. Gokul Nāth was the author of other works, including the *Govind Sukhad Bihār* and the *Chet Chandrikā*, in the latter of which he has described the family history of Rājā Chet Singh, of Benares, who was his patron. His greatest achievement, however, was the translations of the Mahābhārata. In this work he was assisted by his son *Gopī Nāth* and his pupil *Maṇi Dev*.

The Patronage of Courts.—The modern influence on Hindī literature did not spread all at once, and in many places the old state of affairs still continued for some time. The work of the printing-press did not penetrate into all regions immediately, and poets still looked to the rulers of states to help them by their patronage. At the courts of Pannā and Charkhārī in Bundelkhaṇḍ, of Rewah in Baghelkhaṇḍ, of Nagpur, Benares, Ayodhyā, and other principalities, poets and bards were still welcomed and encouraged, and several rulers were themselves poets. Mahārāja *Mān Singh* of Jodhpur (fl. 1810) was the author of various works chiefly in Rājasthānī. *Chandra Śekhar Bājpeyī* (1798-1875), who was at the courts of Darbhangā, Jodhpur and Patiala, excelled in the erotic and heroic styles and was the author of the *Hammir Haṭh* and other works. Mahārāja

Hindūpati, of Pannā, was the patron of *Mohan Bhaṭṭ*, as well as of *Rūp Sāhi* and *Karan* (fl. circ. 1800), the latter being a writer on the art of poetry. Mohan Bhaṭṭ attended other courts also. His son was a well-known poet named Padmākar Bhaṭṭ (see below), who also visited various courts. The Rājās of Charkhārī, named Khumān Singh, Vikram Sāhi, and Ratan Singh, were all great patrons of poets. *Vikram Sāhi* (1785-1828) was himself a successful poet. Among his works is a *Sat Saī*, in imitation of Bihāri Lāl's great work. The poets who attended his court include *Baitāl*, *Mān*, and *Bāl Dev* (all fl. 1820). *Bihārī Lāl*, *Avadhes*, *Rāv Rānā*, *Gopāl*, *Rām Dīn Tripāṭhī* (all fl. 1840) attended the court of Rājā Ratan Singh. *Sūrya Malla* (fl. 1840), who was at the court of the Rājā of Būndī, wrote a long work called the *Banś Bhāskar*, which in the form of illustrative verses gives an account of the Kingdom of Būndī. In Baghelkhaṇḍ, at the court of Rewah, poets were also encouraged both by Mahārāja *Jai Singh* (fl. 1764-1834) and his son *Viśvanāth Singh* (1789-1854). Both these kings not only patronised poets but were themselves authors. Viśvanāth Singh wrote in Sanskrit and Hindī. In Hindī he composed commentaries on the *Bījak* of Kabīr and on the *Vinay Patrikā* of Tulsī Dās, as well as a work entitled *Rām Chandra kī Sawārī*. The poetical traditions of this royal family were also maintained by Viśvanāth's successor, Rājā *Raghu Rāj Singh* (1823-1879), who came to the throne in 1858. He was the author of a much admired translation of the *Bhāgavata Purāṇa* and of a history of Hanumān, entitled *Sundar Śatak*, besides many other works. Mahārāja *Mān Singh* (fl. 1850), of Ayodhyā, was another monarch who was both a poet and a patron of poets.

The Art of Poetry.—Many of the poets who attended the courts of kings were writers on the art of poetry, and this particular form of composition continued to receive great attention. *Gurdīn Pāṇḍe* (fl. 1803) wrote an excellent work on the same lines as Keśav Dās's *Kavi Priyā*. *Benī Pravīn Bājpeyī* (fl. 1817), a Brahman of Lucknow, whose poetry is full of excellent verses, wrote several works connected with the art of poetry. One of the most famous of writers of this period was *Padmākar Bhaṭṭ* (1753-1833), of Bāndā. He attended the courts of various rulers and was richly rewarded for his poetry. He is the reputed author of about seven works, mostly concerning the art of poetry, which are very much praised. One of his outstanding qualities is his skilful use of alliteration. His best work is considered to be the *Jagadvinod* (1810). At the end of his days he is said to have devoted his life to the worship of the Ganges, and wrote a book entitled *Gangā Laharī*. His grandson, *Gadā Dhar Bhaṭṭ* (fl. 1860), was also a poet and wrote on rhetoric. A contemporary and rival of Padmākar was *Gwāl*, of Muttra, who wrote works on the art of poetry. His most famous work is the *Yamunā Laharī*. About the same time or a little later flourished also *Rām Sahāy Dās* (1820), of Benares, and *Pajnes* (1843), of Pannā. The former, who was a poet of considerable merit, took Bihārī Lāl as his model. *Pratāp Sāhi* (fl. 1828) was a devotee of Rāma and the author of several works connected with the art of poetry. In the cleverness of his language he is said to resemble Mati Rām. *Bihārī Lāl Tripāṭhī* (fl. 1840) belonged to a family which has produced many poets, being a descendant of Mati Rām Tripāṭhī. *Navīn* (fl. 1842) wrote several works of high standard on poetics. *Gaṅesh Prasād Farukhābādī* (fl. 1847-1877) was a Kāyasth, of Farukhābād, who wrote a *Nakhśikh* and other works. *Giri Dhar Dās* (fl. 1843) was the father of Hariśchandra. His real name was *Gopāl Chandra*. He wrote about forty different works. *Sardār* (1845-1883), of Benares, and *Nārāyaṇ Rāy* flourished in the second half of the nineteenth century. The former was the author of several works on the art of poetry, including commentaries on the works of *Keśav Dās* and on the *Sat Saī* of Bihārī Lāl, and a commentary on some of the emblematic couplets of Sūr Dās. The *Sṛingār Saṅgrah*, another poem of Sardār, is a popular work on rhetoric, dealing with all branches of the art of poetry. Nārāyaṇ Rāy was a pupil of Sardār. A much admired work in the Māṛwārī dialect is the *Raghunāth Rūpak* of *Manśā Rām*, which was written about the beginning of the nineteenth century. It is a prosody in which the illustrative examples are so arranged that they give a continuous history of the life of Rāma.

Bihari Poets.—A few Bihārī poets of the nineteenth century may be mentioned, all of whom wrote in the Maithilī dialect. *Bhānu Nāth Jhā* (fl. 1850) and *Harsh Nāth Jhā* (born 1847) both attended the court of the Mahārāja of Darbhangā. Bhānu Nāth's best known work is a play entitled *Prabhāvati Haraṇ*. Harsh Nāth wrote many songs as well as plays. A popular account of the famine of 1873-74, entitled *Kavitta Akālī*, was written by *Phatūrī Lāl*, a Kāyasth of Tirhut. *Chandra Jhā*, who flourished in the latter half of the nineteenth century, was the author of a Rāmāyaṇ in Maithilī, which is much admired.

Religious Verse.—Though a great deal of the literature already described has a religious connection the output of religious verse due directly to the various sectarian movements seems to have been less since the beginning of the nineteenth century than in previous times. Contact with the new influences which have come from the West has led indeed to a great deal of religious activity in India, but a large part of the new movements has been in the direction of religious reform. Prose literature, whether in the form of pamphlets or newspapers, has come to be very much used for the dissemination of religious as well as other ideas. Still, the production of poetry in connection with the various religious movemen.s did not entirely cease. In 1806 *Jai Chand*, of Jaipur, wrote a Sanskrit and Hindī work which deals with the doctrines of the Jains, entitled *Svāmī Kārttikeyānupreksha*. A later Jain of considerable merit was *Brindāban Jī* (circ. 1791-1858), of Benares. *Bakhtāwar* (fl. 1817), of Hāthras, in the district of Aligarh, who was a religious mendicant, wrote a book entitled *Sūnīsār*, which was intended to show that all notions of God and man are fallacies and that nothing exists. There were several works also connected with the Rāma cult. *Mān* (fl. 1803) was the author of the *Rām Rāvan Yuddh* and other works dealing with the stories of Rāma. *Lalak Dās* (fl. 1813), of the Lucknow district, wrote the *Satyopākhyān*, which relates the early life of Rāma from his birth to his marriage. The *Rāmāyaṇ* in the Maithilī dialect, composed by *Chandra Jhā*, has already been mentioned. *Sahaj Rām* (born 1804), who lived in the district of Sītāpur, also wrote a *Rāmāyaṇ* which is a translation of the Sanskrit *Raghuvaṁśa* and of the *Hanumān Nāṭaka*. In the latter half of the nineteenth century *Raghu Nāth Dās*, a Brahman of Ayodhyā, wrote hundreds of hymns in honour of Rāma, of whom he was a devotee, while in the same period *Jānkī Prasād*, of the district of Rāe Barelī, wrote several poems dealing with the story of Rāma which are considered to be very excellent. Commentaries also were written on the works of Tulsī Dās, such as the *Mānas Śankāvalī* of *Bandan Pāṭhak*, of Benares, which is a commentary on the *Rāmāyaṇ*, and the *Rām Tattva Bodhanī* of *Śiv Prakāś Singh*, which is a commentary on the *Vinay Patrikā*. These appeared in the latter half of the nineteenth century. Of writers who were devotees of Kṛishṇa the following may be mentioned: *Rasik Govind* (fl. 1801), who wrote works, which are much praised, all connected with the Kṛishṇa legends, and *Lalit Kishorī* (fl. 1860-1873), whose works are also connected with Kṛishṇa and full of merit as works of poetry.

The spread of the Christian faith in India has also been accompanied by the production of Christian hymns. Many of these are translations of English hymns written in English metres, which, judged according to Indian standards, sound barbarous and uncouth. But a large number have also been written in Hindī metres, and many of these have a popularity far beyond the bounds of the Christian Church. Curiously enough, one of the most famous writers of Christian hymns in

Hindī metre was a European named *John Christian* (died about 1883). His most famous work is the *Mukti Muktāvalī*, a life of Christ in verse.

Thus, while the nineteenth century was a period of great change characterised especially by the development of prose literature, and the application of it to a large number of new subjects, literature of the older type still continued to be produced, though it generally exhibited little or no novelty in its themes. The period has been largely a time of transition, and in spite of its many past glories Hindī literature still awaits its more complete development. No attempt is here made to give an account of the writers in prose and poetry of the last thirty or forty years. Many of these writers are still living, and time alone will show how much of their work will have a lasting fame and prove of real value.

XI.

SOME GENERAL CHARACTERISTICS OF HINDĪ LITERATURE

HAVING now traced the history of Hindī literature from its earliest times to the present day, it may be helpful to mention in this chapter some of its general characteristics even at the risk of some repetition of points already mentioned.

1. The first striking feature is that, during the time when it grew and flourished through its own original force, Hindī literature was dominated by a *religious interest.* Probably much more than half of the literature directly springs from the *bhakti* movement in one or other of its aspects. A great deal of the remainder is concerned with the art of poetry; and even in these works the illustrative verses, which form the greater part of them are often connected with one or other of the various religious movements. The bardic chronicles, and some other parts of the literature, are secular in character, but even in these the religious interest is not quite out of sight.

2. Until the beginning of the nineteenth century practically the whole of the literature was in verse. There are indeed a few exceptions. The works ascribed to Gorakhnāth (though almost certainly not by him) include one in prose, and if this is correctly dated as belonging to the fourteenth century it is the earliest Hindī prose work extant. Then we have the *Maṇḍan* of Viṭṭhalnāth and the *Chaurāsī Vārtā* of Gokul Nāth in the sixteenth century, and Dāmodar Dās's translation of the *Mārkaṇḍeya Purāṇa* in the seventeenth century. Besides these, and the commentaries which accom-

panied certain works, there is very little else till we come to the time of Lallū Jī Lāl. Even commentaries were often in the form of poetry. The system of versification was very complicated, but all authors seem to have found it more natural to write verse than prose. When proṣe was first employed, at the beginning of the nineteenth century, writers at first found it more awkward and difficult to manage than poetry. Even text-books on such subjects as veterinary surgery, astronomy or lexicography were written in verse.

3. From about the middle of the sixteenth century the literature became self-conscious, and from the time of Keśav Dās onwards an enormous number of works have appeared dealing with the rules of prosody and the art of poetry generally. Apart from verse of a directly religious character this was indeed the favourite subject of composition amongst Hindī poets. The tendency to lay great stress on the form rather than the substance, and to develop a certain amount of artificiality could not, under such circumstances, be avoided. It is considered a mark of a writer's ability if his words are capable of more than one meaning, and ingenuity of phrase, whether by way of *double entendre*, or alliteration, or any other literary device, is greatly admired. Even nowadays there seems to be a tendency to appraise poets more on account of their technical skill than on account of the message which they have to give. But even so the writers on the art of poetry, who include some of the best Hindī writers, have produced a great deal of verse which is very graceful and artistic, and it must be said that the strict rules as to versification, and their great elaboration, have helped to make Hindī poetry almost unrivalled for melody and rhythm.

4. *Conventionality* in the use of metaphors is another feature of Hindī poetry. Some of these metaphors do not correspond with the facts of nature, but Hindī poets are never tired of repeating them. The separation of the *c̣hakwā* bird from its mate at

night; the eager waiting of the *chātak* bird, who is supposed to drink only raindrops, for the beginning of the rainy season; the *chakor* bird, that is never happy except when gazing on the moon; the swan that knows how to separate milk from the water with which it has been mixed—these and many other stock metaphors are continually recurring in Hindī poets. But many beautiful similes, drawn from a true observation of nature at first hand, are also found not only in the works of Tulsī Dās, but also in the verses of other poets.

5. Another thing to be noticed in Hindī poetry is *the limitation of the range of its subject matter.* Not only is the religious interest dominant, but even in connection with this the subjects dealt with are confined to well-worn grooves. The stories of Rāma and of Kṛishṇa form a very large part of the subject matter and have been told over and over again by poet after poet. There are differences in treatment, but the same details are constantly appearing again and again. Those religious poets who avoid these themes are very largely occupied with such subjects as have already been noted in a previous chapter, namely, the value of the *guru*, the importance of *bhakti*, the evils of transmigration, the deceit of *māyā*, the transitoriness of the world, and suchlike subjects. One misses also the poetry of pure human love. There is indeed a good deal of erotic poetry of a very unhealthy type, but owing to the general practice of child-marriage, and the secluded position occupied by women, the romantic period of youth, which is the time of courtship, does not come into the lot of young men and women in India, and hence when love is described in Hindī poetry it is too often in connection with the courtesan. But the fidelity of Padmāvatī, the wifely devotion of Sītā, and some other stories of the same type must not, on the other hand, be forgotten. There was also a tendency to look to previous writers for themes of poetic inspiration, and if a great poet achieved success in any subject, he was sure to have a large number of imitators. Thus there

are whole realms of human thought in connection with which Hindī writers have contributed nothing, and great as their work has been, the original and stimulating thoughts which Hindī literature contains are confined within a somewhat narrow area.

6. Yet in spite of its limitations Hindī literature has many excellencies, and is worthy of much greater study than it has yet received. It has truly been described as a "garden of delights." It possesses a system and variety of versification which has seldom, if ever, been excelled, and beauties of thought and phrase, and expressions of deep feeling and noble aspiration, abound. It was moreover genuinely popular, and being written in the dialects of the people, and often as a tacit revolt against the literary exclusiveness of the Sanskrit scholars, it appealed to the heart of the people, and reached a very wide audience. Many of its thoughts and expressions have become closely bound up with the life of the people, and a close acquaintance with the vernacular literature is most important for all who would fully understand the peoples of India.

XII.

PRESENT POSITION AND PROSPECTS

WITH such a splendid record of past achievements what is the present position of Hindī literature? What are its prospects of development? A brief answer to these questions is all that can be attempted in this present chapter.

In the first place it is to be noted that Hindī literature has to face many present difficulties, some of which it shares with other Indian vernaculars, and some of which are peculiar to itself. This is not the place to discuss the question whether English or the vernacular should be the medium of instruction in higher education. But it is certainly true that most educated Indian people would be very sorry that their sons should surrender the opportunity which a knowledge of English gives not only of becoming acquainted with the vast stores of Western learning, but of carrying on intercourse with educated people from other parts of India who possess a different vernacular from their own. It is, however, almost unavoidable that such a state of affairs should put Hindī somewhat at a disadvantage, for if a writer wishes to appeal to a widespread educated audience it is natural for him to use English rather than the vernacular to express his ideas, and hence there is sometimes a tendency to despise the vernacular as a medium of literature, and to regard vernacular productions as more intended for the unlearned than for the educated. This is a condition of things in every way to be deplored, and it is to be hoped that, without lessening the opportunities for securing an acquaintance with English, the vernacular may be given a much more important place in the future.

Hindi is also under a disadvantage because its standards of prose have not yet been fixed. We have seen that not only is the prose literature a plant of very recent growth, but that the dialect of High Hindī which it uses is also a modern production. There are scarcely any prose standards of the past to look to, and the present state of the language is transitional. Some authors attempt to write in a language from which are expelled, as far as possible, all words other than those of Hindī or Sanskrit origin. But if this standard be adopted the language is for the common folk very difficult to understand. Other writers go to the opposite extreme and admit a great many words not only of Arabic and Persian, but also of English origin, even when there are simple and well-understood Hindī words which could just as well express their meaning. It seems indeed inevitable that for the expression of modern ideas a good deal of borrowing must take place, but the limits to which this should go can only be settled in course of time by the practice of good prose writers. At present there is a great deal of variation, both in translations and original works, with regard to the language used, and the adoption of some generally recognised standard is very much to be desired.

Owing to Hindī prose literature being written in a modern artificial dialect, which has not proved itself very popular for the purposes of poetry, it has come about not only that the language of poetry is different from that of prose, but that there are several different dialects still used for poetry. The existence of a widely divergent standard between the language of prose and that of poetry would be unfortunate in many ways, and it cannot be said what the ultimate issue of this matter will be, but there does seem a tendency amongst some modern poets to use a language which is approximating more to that of prose.

These disadvantages to the present development of Hindī literature are, however, being counteracted by many favourable circumstances. The spread of education, with the prospect that the day is not far distant when it will be made compulsory, at least for boys, is helping to increase rapidly the number of those who can read. Moreover, the modern tendency to extend the franchise, and to give increased political responsibility to large numbers of the people of India will also make it necessary to acquaint them with various aspects of modern political, social, religious, and other questions. It is impossible with increasing education and enlightenment that a language which can be understood by over a hundred millions of people should not eventually develop a great modern literature, though it may not be easy to forecast the exact lines of its development.

The existence of societies for the extension and improvement of Hindī literature is also a sign of great hope. The *Nāgarī Prachāriṇī Sabhā*, whose headquarters are at Benares, is doing most useful work. It conducts a systematic search for old manuscripts, and publishes many good editions of the older works of Hindī literature. It also issues many useful books in which a high standard is aimed at. It encourages Hindī writers to produce original books and also to translate important books from European languages. Amongst other works it has undertaken the publication of a standard Hindī dictionary in several volumes. Many others also are publishing the works of various Hindī authors, whose works up till now have existed only in manuscript, and have often been hardly known outside the particular sect to which the authors belonged. Translations of many English and other works are being produced in great numbers, making it possible even for those who are unacquainted with English to gain some knowledge of the culture of the West. Moreover, books on subjects connected with politics, science, philosophy, morals, history, and religion are being constantly issued from the press. A great deal of what is produced may not have great value as literature, but it is all helping to cultivate and enlarge the resources of the language to meet the needs of to-day. A Hindī society which has its headquarters at Allahabad is the *Sāhitya Sammelan*, which conducts examinations in Hindī of a very high standard and grants diplomas, and is trying to establish purely Hindī schools in all parts of North and Mid India.

Amongst other societies that are doing much to extend Hindī literature the *North India Tract Society* and other Christian societies hold an important place. Through the agency of these societies a great deal of Hindī literature has been produced not only of a directly religious nature, but also stories, biographies, educational books, and books on social and other subjects. Indian people themselves are often largely unaware how much of the new movements for political freedom, social emancipation, and religious reform are really inspired by Christian ideals. India has seen the vision of a future glory for herself and her children greater even than her past achievements, excellent as these have been. New ideals of righteousness and of duty, of brotherhood and of service have come before her, and inspiration for these has been very largely due to the life and teaching of Christ, who in this as in so many other ways is the fulfilment of all that is noble and excellent in Indian life. The ideas of the old mythology, which formed so large a part of the themes of writers in the past, are on the wane, and the past ideals with regard to many other matters are undergoing a charge. India is seeking out after a larger, a fuller, a more complete life than she has lived in the past. In this development the vernacular literature is bound to have a most important part to play. The responsibility resting upon all writers, where such great issues are at stake, is very great, but the situation is one which should call forth the very best and noblest work from all who are concerned in the production of literature.

BIBLIOGRAPHY

History of the Literature, etc.

The Modern Vernacular Literature of Hindustan. Sir George A. Grierson. 1889. Published by the Asiatic Society of Bengal (Calcutta).

Miśra Bandhu Vinod. (3 vols.) An account in Hindī of the literature, with examples of the work of the chief authors, by the Miśra brothers. Published by the Hindī Granth Prasārak Mandalī (Khaṇḍwā and Allahabad).

Hindī Navaratna. An account in Hindī by the same authors of nine great Hindī writers, *viz.*, Tulsī Dās, Sūr Dās, Dev, Bihārī Lāl, Bhūshaṇ, Keśav Dās, Mati Rām, Chand Bardāī, and Hariśchandra. Publishers as above.

Kavitā Kaumudī. By Rām Naresh Tripāṭhī. Vol. I. deals with the literature down to the time of, but not including, Hariśchandra, and contains an account of 89 poets and gives copious extracts from their work. Vol. II. is not yet published. (Sāhitya Sammelan Office, Allahabad).

Santbānī Saṅgrah. (2 vols.) Contains extracts from the works of thirty-five Hindī religious poets, with notes. (Belvedere Steam Printing Press, Allahabad.)

Encyclopædia Britannica. Edition XI. Vol. XIII. pp. 483-491.

Imperial Gazetteer of India. Vol. II.

Linguistic Survey of India. Sir George A. Grierson. Contains much useful information as to the language and dialects.

The Encyclopædia of Religion and Ethics. Contains articles on several of the different sects whose literature is described in this book.

Translations.

Only a small portion of the vast quantity of Hindī literature has been translated into English. The following are some of the translations (the list is not exhaustive) which have been made, and which in most cases contain also information as to the authors and their work.

Translation of the Rāmāyaṇ of Tulsī Dās. By F. S. Growse.

Mathurā. By F. S. Growse. Contains translations of some of the poems of worshippers of Kṛishṇa.

The Sikh Religion. By M. A. Macauliffe. (6 vols.) Contains a translation of the *Granth* (Clarendon Press).

A History of the Boondelas. By W.R. Pogson. (Calcutta, 1828). A translation of Lāl Kavi's *Chhatra Prakāś.*

The Bījak of Kabīr. Translation into English by the Rev. Ahmad Shāh.

The Padumāvati of Malik Muhammad Jaisī. Edited, with a commentary, translation, and critical notes, by Sir G. A. Grierson and Mahāmahopādhyāya Sudhākar Dvivedī. (Asiatic Society of Bengal, Calcutta.)

Texts.

It is impossible to give a list of all the Hindī texts which have been published, but the following list of publishers of Hindī texts may be of some use. I am indebted for this list to Pandit Śyām Bihārī Miśra, of Allahabad.

1. The Venkateshwar Press, Bombay.
   (Has published a good edition of the *Sūr Sāgar* of Sūr Dās.)
2. The Newal Kishore Press, Lucknow.
3. The Khadga Vilas Press, Bankipore, Bihār.
   (Has published all the available works of Hariśchandra.)
4. The Bharat Jivan Press, Benares City.
   (Has issued works of some well-known Hindī poets.)
5. The Bang Bosi Press, Hindī Bang Bosi Office, Calcutta.
   (Has printed an annotated edition of Bihārī Lāl's *Sat Saī.*)
6. The Nirnaya Sagar Press, Bombay.
7. The Indian Press, Allahabad.
   (Has published a good edition of the *Rāmāyaṇ* of Tulsī Dās.)
8. L. Ram Narain Lal, Publisher and Bookseller, Katra, Allahabad.
9. The Hindī Sāhitya Sammelan Office, Johnston Ganj, Allahabad.
10. The Kāshi Nāgarī Prachāriṇi Sabhā, Benares City.
    (Has published editions of Chand Bardāī's *Rāso*, Tulsī Dās's *Rāmāyaṇ*, Bhūshaṇ's works, and a great many other famous Hindī works.)
11. The Bharat Mitra Press, Calcutta.
12. The Belvedere Steam Printing Press, Allahabad.

INDEX